025.04
CHO

D0302019

1918187

# ORGANIZING INFORMATION
## from the shelf to the web

045. 04
CHO

# ORGANIZING INFORMATION

## from the shelf to the web

**G G Chowdhury and Sudatta Chowdhury**

UNIVERSITY OF WALES, NEWPORT
LIBRARY AND INFORMATION SERVICES CAERLEON

facet publishing

© G G Chowdhury and Sudatta Chowdhury 2007

Published by
Facet Publishing
7 Ridgmount Street
London WC1E 7AE
www.facetpublishing.co.uk

Facet Publishing is wholly owned by CILIP: the Chartered Institute of
Library and Information Professionals.

G G Chowdhury and Sudatta Chowdhury have asserted their right
under the Copyright, Designs and Patents Act 1988 to be identified as
authors of this work.

Except as otherwise permitted under the Copyright, Designs and
Patents Act 1988 this publication may only be reproduced, stored or
transmitted in any form or by any means, with the prior permission of
the publisher, or, in the case of reprographic reproduction, in
accordance with the terms of a licence issued by The Copyright
Licensing Agency. Enquiries concerning reproduction outside those
terms should be sent to Facet Publishing, 7 Ridgmount Street, London
WC1E 7AE.

*British Library Cataloguing in Publication Data*
A catalogue record for this book is available from the British Library.

ISBN 978-1-85604-578-0

First published 2007

Typeset from author's disk in 11/14 pt Bergamo and URW Grotesk by
Facet Publishing.
Printed and made in Great Britian by Cromwell Press Ltd,
Trowbridge, Wiltshire.

To our two wonderful sons

Avirup and Anubhav

# Contents

# Preface

Over the past few years, LIS (library and information science) departments have, for various reasons, reduced their teaching of classification and cataloguing – the essential skills, and the corresponding tools and standards, required for organizing information. Today, very few LIS schools and departments in the UK or abroad offer a full and compulsory course module on information organization. The main argument supporting this move was that libraries could easily get ready-made class numbers and catalogue records for bibliographic resources and hence there was no need to emphasize classification and cataloguing. This is not a very strong or appropriate justification. Given the current state of developments in terms of the internet, the web and digital libraries, the need for organizing information has increased significantly.

In a digital library, more specifically in a hybrid library (a library providing both traditional and digital library services), information professionals need to be prepared for organizing both printed and digital information resources, and in many cases ready-made class numbers and catalogue records are not available (particularly for digital information resources). In fact, quite often LIS professionals have to try to find the most effective means of organizing such information resources themselves. In addition, every organization/institution now produces a great deal of digital information, and their day-to-day activities heavily depend on access to, and use of, the appropriate digital information resources. This reinforces the need for appropriate organization of institutional information resources for better access and management. Indeed, many new approaches, tools and techniques have emerged over the past few years for such activities. It is therefore suggested that tomorrow's LIS professionals should be conversant with these, and with the skills for organizing information in all the different domains – from the traditional to the web and digital library shelf.

This book aims to cover the broad spectrum of information

organization in different environments – from print libraries to the internet, intranet and web. It discusses the tools and techniques and the advantages and disadvantages of various approaches to organizing information. Covering every aspect of these is not possible within a single book. However, this book aims to provide a good coverage of the entire spectrum of information organization which will educate tomorrow's information professionals about the entire field, and will lead interested readers to further studies and research by pointing them to the appropriate references.

Chapter 1 provides a broad overview of the various approaches to organizing bibliographic information. Chapter 2 discusses the range of non-library approaches to organizing information, from the database to the expert systems approach, and various approaches to organizing information on the internet and web. Chapters 3 to 6 discuss the traditional tools and techniques for organizing bibliographic information: Chapter 3 discusses cataloguing, Chapter 4 bibliographic formats, Chapter 5 classification and Chapter 6 subject heading lists and thesauri. Although these tools were primarily designed for organizing bibliographic resources, they have been used by many researchers, subject gateways and digital libraries to organize digital information resources. Examples of some such applications have been provided in each of these chapters.

The major drawbacks of the tools and techniques for bibliographic organization (cataloguing, classification and vocabulary control), which make them rather unsuitable or inappropriate for the organization of digital resources, are discussed in Chapter 7. The new tools, techniques and standards that have emerged over the past few years for organizing digital information, especially the internet and web information resources, are introduced in Chapter 7 and discussed in detail in the subsequent chapters.

Chapter 8 introduces metadata and metadata standards such as Dublin Core and eGMS, and discusses the various management issues related to metadata. Chapter 9 considers markup languages and the evolution of markup languages from SGML to HTML, XML and XHTML. It also discusses the role played by these markup languages in the organization and management of digital information.

Chapter 10 discusses ontology, the new tool designed to facilitate semantic access and retrieval and the management of digital information on the web. The importance of ontologies in the context of content management and the semantic web are also considered in this chapter. Information architecture, the field of study concerned with the organization of web and intranet resources to facilitate the easy access and management of information, is considered in Chapter 11. Chapter 12 discusses the basic concepts of the semantic web – the new vision of the web that will allow computers to understand, retrieve and process information from a variety of sources on the web, primarily on the basis of the semantics, or the meaning, of the information resources concerned. Finally, some major research issues and trends in relation to various aspects of organizing information – traditionally and digitally – are discussed in Chapter 13.

Students in various information science departments – not necessarily only in library and information science programmes but also in a range of other programmes such as information science, information management, information technologies, etc. – will benefit from this book. It will introduce them to the various information organization principles, tools and techniques.

The book can also be used by practising LIS professionals who would like to obtain a complete picture and understanding of how to organize information. If they are interested in any particular area or aspect of information organization, they can follow up the appropriate references that appear at the end of each chapter.

## Acknowledgements

In order to illustrate the content of this book, we have included a number of screenshots of different information systems and services, which are acknowledged below.

Figure 5.1: 'Dewey Services' http://connexion.oclc.org © OCLC
   Online Computer Library Center 11 April 2007
   http://connexion.oclc.org/WebZ/html/corc/corcframe.html?sessionid=
   cnx07.prod.oclc.org-55890-f0dm5gqm-8kaymd:entitydbname=
   DeweyDB?
Figure 5.2: 'Dewey Services' http://connexion.oclc.org © OCLC
   Online Computer Library Center 11 April 2007
   http://connexion.oclc.org/WebZ/html/corc/corcframe.html?sessionid=
   cnx07.prod.oclc.org-55890-f0dm5gqm-8kaymd:entitydbname=
   DeweyDB
Figure 5.3: 'Dewey Services' http://connexion.oclc.org © OCLC
   Online Computer Library Center 11 April 2007

http://connexion.oclc.org/WebZ/DeweyCorcQuery?sessionid=
cnx07.prod.oclc.org-55890-f0dm5gqm-8kaymd

Figure 5.4: 'Dewey Services' http://connexion.oclc.org © OCLC
Online Computer Library Center 11 April 2007
http://connexion.oclc.org/WebZ/DeweyCorcQuery?sessionid=
cnx07.prod.oclc.org-55890-f0dm5gqm-8kaymd?

Figure 5.5: 'BUBL Information Service' © Centre for Digital Library
Research, Strathclyde University, Glasgow G1 1XH, Scotland

Figure 6.5: 'Intute: Health & Life Sciences'
www.intute.ac.uk/healthandlifesciences/browse.html © The Intute
Consortium

Figure 6.6: 'Intute: Health & Life Sciences'
www.intute.ac.uk/healthandlifesciences/medicine/mesh_a.html
© The Intute Consortium

Figure 6.7: 'Intute: Social Sciences' www.intute.ac.uk/socialsciences/
© The Intute Consortium

Figure 6.8: 'Intute: Social Sciences' www.intute.ac.uk/socialsciences/
cgi-bin/browse.pl?id=120274 © The Intute Consortium

Figures 12.1 and 12.2: RDF model reproduced from the RDF Primer
available at www.w3.org/TR/rdf-primer/#conceptsummary

Many individuals and institutions have directly or indirectly helped us in
preparing this book. Those whose resources have been used as illustrations
are acknowledged with thanks. We are also grateful to the reviewers who
made useful comments on earlier drafts of the book.

We are indebted to several members of our family – with special thanks
to our two sons Avirup and Anubhav – who have provided encourage-
ment and inspiration throughout this project. Finally we would like to
express our gratitude to the staff of Facet Publishing, especially to Helen,
Lin and Kathryn for their kind help and support at every stage of our
work on the book.

G. G. Chowdhury and
Sudatta Chowdhury

# Glossary

**AACR2** *Anglo-American Cataloguing Rules*, 2nd edition. This publication provides comprehensive guidelines for the preparation of catalogue entries and is used as a *de facto* standard in the context of library **catalogues**.

**analytico-synthetic classification** A classification scheme that to some extent is **enumerative** and at the same time makes provision for some sort of synthesis to build the class number. Example: **Universal Decimal Classification (UDC)**.

**array** A set of co-ordinate classes (or sub-classes) all derived by applying the same principle of division to the superordinate class.

**associative relationship** In the context of **vocabulary control**, this denotes the relationship between a pair of terms that are neither **hierarchical** nor **equivalent**, and yet they are associated to such an extent that their relationship should be made explicit.

**BC** Bibliographic Classification. This classification scheme was originally devised by Henry Evelyn Bliss; the first four volumes (Bliss Bibliographic Classification) were published in the USA between 1940 and 1953. The revised edition (BC2) was initiated by Jack Mills and was produced in 22 parts; further revisions have been made to some of the volumes in order to retain subject currency, and the publication is now undertaken by Bowker.

**bibliographic classification** A system of organizing information where the subject divisions are assigned a **notation** or a code that indicates subject content. Examples: **Dewey Decimal Classification (DDC)**, **Universal Decimal Classification (UDC)**, **Colon Classification (CC)**, etc.

**bibliographic format** A standard format that prescribes the various data elements to be used to create a record for a bibliographic item, and thus it governs the process of record creation and exchange. Example: **MARC 21**, **CCF**, etc.

**bibliography** A list of books and other information resources – by or on a given author, in a given subject, etc. – arranged in a specific order.

**BT** Broader term. In the context of the **hierarchical** structure of a **vocabulary control tool** like a **thesaurus** or a **subject heading list**, a broader term denotes a superordinate term, or a term of higher order in the hierarchy in comparison to another term.

**catalogue** A list of, and index to, the information resources in a library or a collection. A catalogue lets the user know details of a library's collection, i.e. it indicates what items the library holds on a given subject, by a given author, etc., and where to locate them.

**catalogue codes** Tools devised to provide rules and guidelines for preparing library catalogues to meet the objectives of **cataloguing**. Example: **AACR2**.

**cataloguing** The act of creating **catalogue** records; sometimes used synonymously (albeit loosely) with **indexing**.

**CC** Colon Classification. Devised by S. R. Ranganathan, this is an example of a **faceted classification** scheme. The seventh edition of Colon Classification, which came out in 1987, provides extreme flexibility in building class numbers of subjects through the principles of **facet** analysis.

**CCF** Common Communications Format. A **bibliographic format** that was developed in order to facilitate the exchange of bibliographic data between organizations; it was first published by UNESCO in 1984, and then in 1988 and 1992.

**class number (or classmark)** A **notational** code, designed to represent the subject content of an information resource, and used to specify its location in a library's collection.

**classification** The process of organizing things in a systematic order. In the context of libraries, classification is a process whose purpose is to (1) specify the location of every bibliographic item on the library's shelves, and (2) display the subject relationships among various bibliographic items in a library's collection.

**classification scheme** A tool for systematic organization of information resources. A classification scheme helps a classifier to represent the subject content of every document in a collection by appropriate **notations**.

**complex subject** A subject formed by the combination of two concepts, usually from different main classes: e.g. 'Statistics for librarians', 'The influence of the internet on child behaviour', etc.

**compound subject** A subject formed by the combination of two or more concepts from the same main class, e.g. 'Rural economics', 'Inorganic acids', etc.

**DAML+OIL** DARPA Agent Markup Language and Ontology Interchange Language. DAML+OIL is a joint name for the US DAML-ONT (DAML Ontology) and the European language (OIL). It was taken as the starting point for the W3C Working Group on Web Ontology in defining **OWL**, the standard and broadly accepted **ontology** language of the **semantic web**.

**database** A collection of logically organized and related data that can be accessed by multiple users to meet their information needs.

**DBMS** Database management system. A software application system that is used to create, maintain and provide controlled access to databases.

**DCMI** The Dublin Core Metadata Initiative.

**DDC** Dewey Decimal Classification. Devised by Melvyl Dewey and first published in 1876, it is currently in its 22nd edition published by **OCLC** in both print and web versions. It is the most widely used library **classification** system in the world.

**digital library** An information service based on the assemblage of digital content and the appropriate tools, techniques and standards, including the computing, storage and communications machinery and software needed to reproduce, emulate and extend the services provided by conventional print-based libraries.

**DTD** document type definition. An **SGML** or **XML** application that is used to define the structure of a particular type of document.

**Dublin Core** A format for **metadata** that defines a core set of 15 data elements that can be used as containers for metadata. The **Dublin Core Metadata Initiative (DCMI)** began in 1995; the first meeting took place at Dublin, Ohio, giving rise to a metadata format called the Dublin Core.

**EAD** Encoded Archival Description. A **metadata** standard that defines the structural elements and designates the content of descriptive guides to archival and manuscript holdings.

**eGMS** e-Government Metadata Standard. This lays down the elements, refinements and encoding schemes to be used by UK government staff when creating **metadata** for information resources.

**enumerative classification**  A **classification** scheme in which all the possible classes are enumerated according to certain characteristics. Example: **Library of Congress Classification (LC)**.

**equivalence relationship**  In the context of **vocabulary control**, this is a relationship between a pair of terms where one is a preferred term (i.e. an index entry can be made under that term) and another a non-preferred term (i.e. an index entry cannot be made under that term; instead a reference entry is made to direct the user to the preferred term).

**expert systems**  Computer systems that embody knowledge about a specific problem domain and can solve problems from the domain using its knowledge with a degree of expertise that is comparable to that of a human expert.

**facet**  A generic term used to denote a component of a subject.

**faceted classification**  A **classification** scheme that, instead of listing all the classes and the corresponding numbers, lists the various **facets** of every subject or main class and provides a set of rules for constructing class numbers through facet analysis.

**folksonomy**  Also known as ethnoclassification. An internet-based information organization method consisting of collaboratively generated, open-ended labels that categorize content such as web pages, online photographs and web links.

**FRBR**  Functional Requirements of Bibliographic Records. Developed under the auspices of **IFLA**, this is a framework for relating the data elements in bibliographic records to the needs of the users of those records.

**fundamental categories**  Proposed by S. R. Ranganathan, these are the building blocks of **facet** analysis. According to Ranganathan, the constituent components of any compound subject can be the manifestation of one of the five fundamental categories: Personality, Matter, Energy, Space and Time, famously known as PMEST.

**hierarchical relationship**  In the context of **vocabulary control** this is a relationship where a pair of terms are represented in their superordinate-subordinate status to show whole-part, thing-kind, genus-species or item-instance relationships.

**hospitality**  In the context of **classification**, this is a property of

**notation** that denotes the capacity of a classification scheme to accommodate new subjects, classes or sub-classes.

**HTML** HyperText Markup Language. HTML is a formal recommendation by the **World Wide Web Consortium** (**W3C**) and is generally adhered to by the major browsers like Internet Explorer and Netscape Navigator. HTML markup tells the web browser how to display a web page's content – text, image, etc. – for the user.

**HTTP** HyperText Transfer Protocol.

**IA** Information architecture. An area of study that is concerned with the organization and labelling of websites, intranets, online communities and software to support usability and findability.

**ICCP** International Conference on Cataloguing Principles. Held in Paris, 9-18 October 1961, and also known as the **Paris Principles**.

**IFLA** International Federation of Library Associations and Institutions.

**indexing** The process of creating an index, i.e. access points for information resources; sometimes used synonymously (albeit loosely) with cataloguing.

**information retrieval** Covers all activities related to the organization, processing and access to information in all forms and formats.

**ISBD** International Standard Bibliographic Description.

**LC** Library of Congress Classification. This was mainly constructed for the Library of Congress (LC) from 1901 onwards, but is also used widely in other libraries throughout the world. It is an **enumerative** classification and provides a long list of all classes of subjects in the universe.

**LCSH** Library of Congress Subject Headings. This was originally designed as a controlled **vocabulary** for representing the subject and form of the books and serials in the Library of Congress collection, with the objective of providing subject access points to the bibliographic records contained in the library's catalogues. It is now the most widely used tool for assigning **subject headings** to bibliographic information resources.

**library catalogue** An organized set of records of the bibliographic information resources in a library's collection.

**library classification** *see* **Bibliographic classification**.

**LIS** Library and information science.

**literary warrant** In the context of information organization, this is a concept that suggests that a new class or heading will be introduced in a tool to represent a topic only when there is a demand, i.e. when an information resource exists that embodies the topic concerned.

**main class** In the context of **classification**, this is one of the primary divisions produced by a **classification scheme**.

**main entry** In the context of **cataloguing**, this is a **catalogue** record that contains the complete catalogue entry for the bibliographic item concerned.

**MARC** MAchine-Readable Catalogue.

**MARC 21** A **bibliographic format** that provides a set of codes and content designators and guidelines for managing and formatting electronic records of information resources.

**metadata** Structured data about information resources (mainly in digital form) that can be used to help support a wide range of operations, such as resource description and discovery, and management of information resources and their long-term preservation.

**metadata standard** Metadata formats designed for creating **metadata** for materials in a specific domain or for materials of a specific kind and format, etc.

**mnemonics** In the context of **classification** this is a property of **notation** that acts as an aid to memory; a mnemonic notation should be easy to remember.

**notation** A symbol that is used to represent a subject or a class in a **classification** scheme.

**NT** Narrower term. In the context of the **hierarchical** structure of a **vocabulary control tool** like a **thesaurus** or a **subject heading list**, a narrower term denotes a subordinate term, or a term of lower order in the hierarchy in comparison to another term.

**OAI** Open Archives Initiative.

**OCLC** Online Computer Library Center.

**online databases** Traditional online databases and online searching denote information searches that are conducted by means of a local computer that communicates with a remote computer system containing bibliographic and/or full-text databases. It is also used as a generic term to denote any **databases** of information resources.

**ontology** A formal, explicit specification of a shared conceptualization. A formal ontology is a controlled **vocabulary** expressed in an ontology representation language that has a grammar and formal constraints specifying how the vocabulary terms can be used.

**OPAC**  Online public access catalogue.

**OWL**  Web Ontology Language.

**page layouts**  Also called wireframes, blueprints or screen details; they define page level navigation, content types and functional elements and are useful in conveying the general page structure and content requirements for individual pages on a website.

**page templates**  In the context of **information architecture**, these are templates that are used to define large-scale websites and intranets; they define the layout of common page elements such as navigation and content.

**Paris Principles**  These define the objectives of a library **catalogue**. The objectives of **cataloguing** proposed by C. A. Cutter in 1876 were modified by Lubetzky and were accepted internationally at the International Conference on Cataloguing Principles held in Paris in 1961; they are known as the **ICCP** Paris Principles.

**personas**  In the context of **information architecture**, these are hypothetical archetypes for actual users created through a series of interviews of the users of a system.

**phase relations**  Relationships between the components of a **complex subject**.

**post-coordinate indexing**  An **indexing** system where one entry is prepared for each keyword selected to represent the subject of a given document, and all the entries are organized in a file; when a user submits a query, individual query terms are matched against the file and documents with matching terms are retrieved.

**pre-coordinate indexing**  An **indexing** system where candidate keywords for every document are chosen and arranged (coordinated) in a specific order to create the index; when a user submits a query, the query terms are matched with the pre-coordinated index strings for matching and retrieval. **Subject heading lists** are examples of pre-coordinate indexing systems.

**prototypes**  In the context of **information architecture**, these are quick designs to elicit user feedback and identify problems, if any exist.

**RDBMS**  Relational database management system. This is a **DBMS** that stores data in the form of tables where the rows represent database objects (records) and columns the characteristics or attributes of those objects. Examples: Access, Oracle.

**RDF** Resource description framework.

**RDF schema** This provides a model for organizing web objects into **hierarchies** by supplying properties, subproperty and subclass relationships, and domain and range restrictions.

**RT** Related term. In the context of the **hierarchical** structure of a **vocabulary control tool** like a **thesaurus** or a **subject heading list**, a related term denotes a co-ordinate term, or a term of same order in the hierarchy in comparison to another term.

**search engine** An **information retrieval** system designed to provide access to electronic information in standalone or networked computer systems, especially on the web.

**semantic web** A term coined by the creator of the web, Tim Berners-Lee, to describe a process whereby data on the web will be defined and linked in such a way that it can be used by machines not only for display purposes, but for the processing, integration and re-use of data across various applications.

**semantic web portal** A web portal based on **semantic web** technology, especially **ontology**.

**SGML** Standard Generalized Markup Language. This is a standard markup language for marking text documents so that they can be processed by computers independently of software and hardware differences.

**site maps** In the context of **information architecture**, these are high level diagrams showing the **hierarchy** of a system that reflects the information structure of an organization.

**storyboards** In the context of **information architecture**, these are sketches showing how a user would interact with a system to complete a common task.

**subject heading list** An alphabetical list of terms and phrases, with appropriate cross-references and notes, that can be used as a source of headings in order to represent the subject content of an information resource. Example: **Library of Congress Subject Headings (LCSH)**.

**subject indexing** The process of creating an **index** based on the subject content of information resources.

**taxonomy** A collection of controlled **vocabulary** terms organized into a **hierarchical** structure where each term is in one or more parent-child relationships to other terms in the collection.

**TEI** Text Encoding Initiative. TEI guidelines for Electronic Text Encoding and Interchange were first published in 1994; they specify a set of tags which may be inserted to mark the textual structure and other features of interest in the text.

**thesaurus** An organized set of controlled **vocabulary** terms showing synonyms, and **hierarchical** and other relationships and dependencies that are used for the indexing and retrieval of information.

**UDC** Universal Decimal Classification. First developed in 1905, this **analytico-synthetic classification** scheme is now one of the most widely used **classification** schemes in the world.

**UNIMARC** UNIversal MARC. In 1977 IFLA brought out the UNIMARC format, whose primary purpose is to facilitate the international exchange of data in machine-readable form between national bibliographic agencies.

**URI** Uniform resource identifier. This is a generic term for all types of names and addresses that refer to information objects on the world wide web.

**URL** Uniform resource locator; simply speaking, an address of a web resource.

**URN** URN, or uniform resource name, is a URI that identifies a resource by a name. As opposed to URL, it simply gives the name of the resource – but does not say how to locate or obtain it.

**VLE** Virtual learning environment.

**vocabulary control tool** An organized list of terms and phrases that can be used to index and search a collection by subject terms and phrases. **Subject heading lists**, e.g. the **Library of Congress Subject Headings (LCSH)**, and **thesauri**, e.g. the UNESCO Thesaurus, are examples of **vocabulary control** tools.

**W3C** World Wide Web Consortium.

**WebDewey** The web version of the **Dewey Decimal Classification (DDC)** scheme.

**XML** eXtensible Markup Language.

**XML schema** A language for describing the structure and constraints to which **XML** documents must conform.

# 1
# Organizing information: what it means

## Introduction

Users in today's world can obtain access to information from a variety of sources through a wide range of channels, from conventional bibliographic resources like books, journals, etc. that can be accessed through OPACs (online public access catalogues), to a myriad of electronic resources. These include online databases, e-journals and e-books, not to mention a host of internet and web resources, each of which can be accessed through specific search interfaces designed by the service providers concerned. One of the major challenges facing library and information professionals and service providers today is how best to organize these information resources, available as they are in their widely differing forms and formats. Libraries and information services have long practised a number of techniques for organizing information resources of various kinds, but the proliferation of digital material is bringing in new challenges every day, and demanding new and improved tools and techniques. In order to understand how information resources of different kinds are organized and the corresponding benefits of doing so – as well as the pitfalls – it is necessary to review some basics. This chapter begins with a broad overview of the various approaches to organizing bibliographic and non-bibliographic information. It then addresses some fundamental issues such as what we mean by the term 'organization', why and how we organize things, what the terms 'classification' and 'cataloguing' mean in the context of our everyday life, and so on. It goes on to provide a brief introduction to the concepts of bibliographic classification, cataloguing and subject indexing.

## Information services in today's world

A typical information user in today's digital world can access information resources and services through a variety of channels, such as:

- library OPACs (online public access catalogues), which provide access to library collections
- online bibliographic or full-text databases (database search services) such as Dialog (www.dialog.com), Ovid (www.ovid.com), ABI/Inform (www.proquest.com/products_pq/descriptions/abi_inform.shtml), etc., which provide access to remote collections
- e-books and e-journal services such as NetLibrary (www.netlibrary.com/), Emerald (www.emeraldinsight.com), Ingenta (www.ingenta.com), etc., which provide access to electronic books and journal articles
- intranets and databases created by companies and institutions to provide access to various information resources within the institution
- websites, which are accessible either by going directly to the site if the web address or URL (uniform resource locator) is known, or by using search tools:
  - search engines like Google (www.google.com)
  - metasearch engines, which collate information from more than one search engine, examples being Dogpile (www.dogpile.com) and Mamma (www.mamma.com)
  - speciality search engines that use special techniques for search and/or display of results, such as Kartoo (www.kartoo.com) and Vivisimo (www.vivisimo.com)
  - directories like Yahoo! (www.yahoo.com)
- subject gateways that provide access to selected web resources in one or more specific discipline(s) such as Intute: social sciences (www.intute.ac.uk/socialsciences/), Intute: arts & humanities (www.intute.ac.uk/artsandhumanities/) and Intute: health & life sciences (www.intute.ac.uk/healthandlifesciences/medicine/)
- digital libraries like the ACM (American Computing Machinery) digital library (http://portal.acm.org/dl.cfm), the New Zealand Digital Library (NZDL; www.nzdl.org) and the (Networked Digital Library of Theses and Dissertations (NDLTD; www.ndltd.org).

Library and information services have, over the years, developed and used various special tools, techniques and standards for organizing information resources. The main objective of the information organization activity in libraries was to facilitate easy access to shelved information resources, although there were other (secondary) objectives, too; for example to facilitate resource sharing. 'Conventional' information organization tools and standards have been used in the library world quite successfully for a long time, but the appearance of digital information resources over the past few decades has brought new challenges to information organization and access (Chowdhury, 2004a, 2004b). Organizing digital information is a complex task, and often the conventional bibliographic tools are not adequate for the purpose.

This book aims to provide an overview of the different approaches to organizing information – including the corresponding tools, techniques and standards – in different forms and formats, ranging from books on the library's shelf to digital information resources accessible through the web and digital libraries. Figure 1.1 (overleaf) provides a generic overview of the various approaches to organizing bibliographic and non-bibliographic information. Conventional approaches to organizing information are briefly introduced in this chapter; the various other approaches to organizing information are introduced in Chapter 2. Thus, together, the first two chapters of this book provide a broad outline of the various library and non-library approaches to organizing information.

## Organization of information: what and why?

Let's begin with a simple, and yet very pertinent, question: why do we organize things? According to the *Oxford English Dictionary* (2006), the term 'to organize' means: 'To arrange into a structured whole; to systematize; to put into a state of order; to arrange in an orderly manner, put in a particular place or order, tidy'.

Note the terms 'to systematize', 'state of order', 'orderly manner', etc. Through organization we generate a working order of items, or arrange items in a system so that we can find and retrieve them as and when necessary without great difficulty.

Telephone directories and the *Yellow Pages* are two very common and simple sources of information that we use frequently in everyday life. Let's take a closer look at these two sources and try to understand how they organize information. Both provide more or less similar information: name, address, telephone number, etc. Both organize information so that users can find the required information easily. Yet there is a significant difference in their approach to organizing information. The entries in a telephone directory contain name, address and telephone number of people, institutions, etc., and the entries are arranged alphabetically by

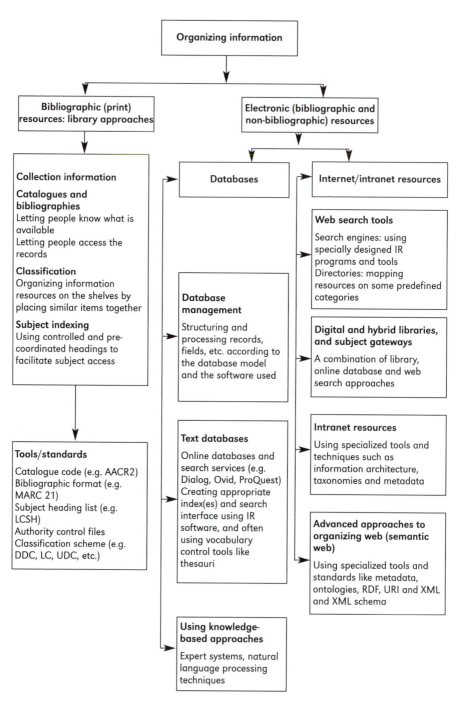

**Figure 1.1** Organization of information: an outline

name. However, although the *Yellow Pages* provides similar information (name, address, contact details, etc., various businesses), its entries are arranged first by the type or category of business, and then alphabetically by name within that category. In some cases, there are subcategories under a specific category; for example in the *Yahoo! Yellow Pages* (2006), some of the categories and sub-categories are:

**Automotive**
   Dealers, motorcycles, repair
**Food and dining**
   Catering, grocers, restaurants
**Legal and financial**
   Banks, insurance, law firms
**Travel and transportation**
   Hotels, taxis, travel agents
etc.

Thus, in both the telephone directory and the *Yellow Pages*, we can find the addresses, contact details, etc., of people or organizations/businesses, but the specific needs for which we use these sources are somewhat different; hence the approach to organizing the entries differs. When we use a telephone directory we usually know the name of the person or institution we are looking for, and thus the entries are arranged alphabetically by name. On the other hand, we use the *Yellow Pages* to find contact details for a person or a business that deals with a specific product or item; hence the main entries are organized by type of business.

We organize things so that we can find them again easily. We also organize things so that we can manage them properly, especially large collections of items – for example so we know (and can let other people know) what we have in a collection or store. The process of organizing of items takes place in all walks of life, consciously or unconsciously. Sometimes we organize items mentally; in other cases we use a formal method or approach that has been laid down and agreed on by stake-holders.

At home, at work and in clubs, bars, shops and restaurants – everywhere – we organize items in a manner that facilitates their easy identification and retrieval. We also do something else – especially when we have a large collection of items and therefore we cannot rely on memory to remember them exactly – we keep a record of each item in our possession so that at any point in time we can check what items we have, how many items we have, how many similar or dissimilar items we have, and so on.

## Classification

Classification is a simple mental process, and is used consciously or unconsciously in all walks of life. Maltby (1975) comments that classification lies at the base of every well managed life and occupation. In the words of Hunter (2002, 2), '[W]herever one looks, examples of the use of classification can be found.' Simply speaking, classification is the process of organizing things in a systematic order. It is the process by which the mind identifies an item and at the same time distinguishes it from others. Often we classify things unconsciously in the course of everyday life. For example, by the process of classification we can identify a car and distinguish it from other cars or other kinds of automobiles, we can identify a bird and distinguish it from other types of birds, we can distinguish one type of animal from another, we can identify and distinguish one group of products from another in a super-market, and so on.

Thus, we may say that classification is the process of arranging things in order of their degrees of likeness, and therefore by analogy separating things according to their degrees of unlikeness. Indeed, classification is the key to knowledge: '[I]f we arrange things in a definite order and we know what that order is, we have a very good map of, or key to, these things' (Maltby, 1975, 16).

So how do we classify things, and is it always the same process irrespective of things and/or their use? Let's look at a simple classification process. How do we distinguish one car from another? Well, there are different characteristics that can be used to group cars, such as the make, model, colour, engine size, year of registration, price, etc. So, in effect, we look for some specific characteristics of the items being classified and group the items based on those characteristics. This means that the way we classify cars cannot be used to classify other objects, such as houses or computers, because the characteristics of the items differ.

Thus, while organizing objects we group them based on their characteristics. But do we always use the same characteristics to organize similar objects, irrespective of the circumstances or the intended use of the objects? Let's take a simple example. We all have shoes at home, and of course there are large shoe stores with hundreds or thousands of pairs of shoes. Do we take the same approaches to organizing shoes at home and in shops? At home we usually organize shoes by owner, type and intended use (school, office, sports, party, etc.). The process gets more complicated if you have too many pairs of shoes at home, even worse if you have bought different pairs to go with different types and colours of dresses, and worst if you are like Imelda Marcos, the former First Lady of the Philippines, and have thousands of pairs of shoes! In a large shop, shoes are grouped by the type (men, women, boys or girls), purpose (school, sports, summer, etc.), brand, size, colour, price, etc.; sometimes shoes that are in a sale or special promotion are kept separately; and in addition, shops use a barcode to identify uniquely each type of shoe and its characteristics, some of which may not be useful for the customers and are meant for the management of the store and the business.

Let's take another example. In a supermarket items are organized (classified to be more precise) by their nature and characteristics: bakery products, meat products, fruits and vegetables, health and beauty products and so on. In addition, supermarkets often keep certain items or products at convenient locations: some sweets and medicine near the checkouts, or Christmas trees and lights near the entrance during the festive season. The main objective of this sort of classification of items is to help customers find required items easily.

So, for classification we use those characteristics of objects that are specifically useful for their identification (and for their distinction from one another) by the intended users. In the process of classifying objects we repeatedly look at the characteristics of those objects, and thus form smaller and smaller groups at each stage. By this repeated process of subdivision, we form smaller groups of similar items at each stage, and the process continues until we reach a stage where all the items have similar characteristics and cannot be subdivided any further. Classification thus creates a hierarchy of classes: objects in a class possess similar characteristics, and are different from those in another class. In other words, a classification process is based on the degree of likeness of similar objects, and the degree of unlikeness of dissimilar objects.

## Purpose of classification

We have already noted that through classification we can organize things and this helps us in:

- identifying things that have similar characteristics
- separating things that have dissimilar characteristics.

So, what is the purpose of having a classification system? Most importantly it helps us to keep related items together, and thus by analogy to keep unrelated items apart. Consequently a classification system helps to locate a specific item in a collection. We have already noted that we use the specific characteristics of the items in a collection to classify them. Therefore, there is another important purpose of classification: it helps us organize items in an order, so that the relationships among the items can be ascertained, and thus we can build a mental map of the items in a collection.

## Cataloguing

We use different types of catalogue in everyday life. Perhaps product catalogues are the most commonly used; for example, the Argos catalogue in Britain or online catalogues of various products. So, why do we use these tools, and what do we expect to find?

'A catalogue is a list of the contents of a particular collection of objects and is arranged in some definite order so as to facilitate the use of that collection, and as a guide to its scope and content' (Corbett, 1966, 297).

When we look at a printed or online catalogue, we expect to get a complete list of all the products available. These products are organized in a definite order so that we can easily find one or more desired items. When we consult a catalogue we expect to find whether or not a particular product or item is available in the collection. We may also like to find how many types of a specific item are available, for example how many types of digital camera or PlayStation games are available. Once we locate an item we then look at its specific entry in order to get more information about the item concerned.

## Purpose of cataloguing

From the perspective of the customer, a catalogue:

- provides information about every item in the collection
- provides the necessary details of each item
- arranges all the entries in a convenient order, so that it is easy to find an item.

From the business perspective, a catalogue tells customers about the items available and thus promotes business.

The two main challenges for the business that produces the catalogue are: to decide what sort of information should be provided about items (the complexity increases when the collection contains different types or categories of items), and to decide how to organize entries so that customers can find items easily. There are other challenges too; for example, how to update the catalogue (i.e. add, delete or edit entries) and, in today's ICT (information and communication technology) environ-ment, how to enter and process the data so that entries can be generated to be used in print and/or electronic form, and the data can be transferred among various agencies for various management reasons.

## Library approaches to organizing information

Libraries have long been using various tools and techniques to organize information resources on the shelves, and to provide means for locating information resources based on various search keys such as subject, title, author, etc. The first approach to the systematic organization and recording of information resources in a library can be traced back to the Library of Alexandria in ancient Egypt. The first catalogue of information resources in the Library of Alexandria was created by the poet and author Callimachus of Cyrene (305–235 BC), who was a librarian at Alexandria. Cataloguing of library resources developed much later in western Europe; modern library catalogues date back to the French Code of 1791, and cataloguing rules developed by Panizzi were published in 1841 (Hanson and Daily, 1970; Svenonius 2000).

## Bibliographic classification

Library classification (also called bibliographic classification) systems aim to achieve two main objectives:

- to specify the location of every bibliographic item on the library's shelves, or in other words to help users locate the required information resources
- to display the subject relationships among various bibliographic items in a collection.

In order to meet these objectives, library classification systems follow two very important principles:

- the principle of ordering of subjects: bibliographic items are arranged on the library's shelves (by their subject content) in the order of general to specific
- the principle of relative location: the items on a library's shelves should not have a fixed location but instead a relative location; each item will have a location in relation to the (subject of) other items in the collection.

In order to achieve the potential of library classification, one has to place each bibliographic item in its most specific subject class. The process of library classification has been nicely summed up by Maltby (1975, 20):

> Within each major subject field, the sequence should begin with general material and proceed slowly to more specialized branches of the subject, the exact order of progression being determined by an accurate analysis of the subject of books and by observing the needs of the majority of specialist readers in each field of activity.

Thus, while a classifier has to determine, and assign, the most specific class to every book in a library, the task of classification should also be guided by the needs of the users; i.e. an information resource should not only be placed under the most specific subject, it should also be placed in a class that will suit the needs of the majority of its users.

One may ask how we should decide the specific subject or class of a given information resource. According to Ranganathan (1962), the specific subject class of a document is the division of knowledge that has an extension and intension equal to its content. In other words, when we classify a document, we should assign a subject that best represents its content – neither a broader class nor a narrower class. Let's take an example: books on information retrieval should be classed under information retrieval, and not under a broader subject such as information or library science; similarly, a book discussing the various models of information retrieval should be classed under information retrieval models (or even under specific models such as the probabilistic, the vector-space or the natural language processing model) and not under the broader subject of information retrieval or information science.

Bibliographic classification systems such as Dewey Decimal Classification (DDC) bring related information resources together, and by analogy keep unrelated information resources apart. In other words, library classification systems allow us to keep all the resources on a given subject, say economics or chemistry, together. They also allow us to keep items on related subjects like law, politics, etc., close together, as opposed to subjects that are not related such as history and physics. Library classification schemes are primarily used for shelf location; they specify the order of arrangement of information resources on the library's shelves.

Modern classification schemes such as DDC, Universal Decimal Classification (UDC), Library of Congress Classification (LC), Colon Classification (CC), etc. were devised several decades ago or more. Although over the years they have been modified and improved, their main objective has remained unchanged – to enable libraries to denote the content of every document by some notation which can be used to specify a shelf location. Classification schemes enable users to locate a given information resource among millions of documents in a collection – for example, in a large national library like the Library of Congress or The British Library.

Library classification schemes can be used to classify any type of information resource – books, journal articles, conference papers, maps, video cassettes, etc. The features of selected classification schemes are discussed in Chapter 5.

## Catalogues and bibliographies

Library classification schemes help us allocate a specific class number and thus specify a shelf location for an information resource. Library catalogues help users find information resources. A catalogue is a list of, and index to, the information resources in a library or a collection. In the *Encyclopedia of Library and Information Science*, a catalogue is defined as 'a list of books contained within a single library and is comprehensive rather than selective' (Hanson and Daily, 1970, 242). This definition emphasizes that a library catalogue provides a complete list of a library's collection. A more comprehensive definition is provided by *Elsevier's Dictionary of Library Science, Information and Documentation* (1973), where a catalogue has been defined as 'an ordered compilation of item descriptions and sufficient information to afford access to entries'. Thus a catalogue lets the user know about a library's collection: what the library has on a given subject, by a given author, etc. It is also important to note that a catalogue should provide all the information necessary to obtain access to the item concerned.

Hanson and Daily (1970) comment that a substantial relationship exists between a catalogue and a bibliography. According to the *Oxford English Dictionary* (2006) a bibliography is 'a list of the books of a particular author, printer, or country, or of those dealing with any particular theme; the literature of a subject'. As in a catalogue, an entry in a bibliography provides all the information necessary to access a particular information resource. This is evident from the following definition in *Harrod's Librarian's Glossary* (Prytherch, 2005, 66), where a bibliography has been defined thus: 'The compilation of systematic or enumerative bibliographies – books, MSS, audio-visual formats and other publications arranged in a logical order giving author, title, date and place of publication, publisher, details of edition, pagination, series, and literary/information contents'.

The difference between a catalogue and a bibliography is that while a catalogue provides records of the collection of a particular library (or sometimes a group of libraries), a bibliography provides records of a collection that is not limited to any one particular library. A bibliography may have been created to record most or all of the items available in a given subject, or produced by a given author or a publisher, or all the items published in a given country, and so on.

The process of cataloguing – defined simply as the art of preparing catalogues – produces different access points and thus allows users to look for items using different keys such as author name, title, publisher, etc.

The process of cataloguing consists of two basic operations: creating entries for every item in the library/collection, and organizing the entries to produce the catalogue (Hunter and Bakewell, 1991).

Thus classification and cataloguing complement each other by providing mechanisms for organizing information resources on a library's shelves, and providing the means for users to search for those items using various search keys. Standard cataloguing tools, called catalogue codes, such as AACR2, or the *Anglo-American Cataloguing Rules*, create catalogue records and achieve the objectives of cataloguing. Details of cataloguing, as well as the corresponding tools and standards, are discussed in Chapter 3.

## Subject heading lists

Library classification schemes help us allocate a specific class number to an information resource so that it can be placed at a particular location on the library's shelves. This helps users find a specific information resource or related information resources. But how would a user know where to look for items on a given subject, say e-commerce, digital photography, or travel and tourism? Clearly, it is not possible for every user to learn and remember the notations used by library classification schemes. Librarians have long used a tool to resolve this problem: subject heading lists (like the Library of Congress Subject Headings, discussed in Chapter 6). These defined terms provide a verbal representation of their subjects and are used as index terms by users to facilitate their search. Users can search by the appropriate subject headings, such as e-commerce or chemical engineering, and once they find a match they note down the corresponding class number that points them to a specific location on the library's shelves. Thus, a combination of classification schemes and subject heading lists helps librarians organize information resources on the library's shelves and helps users find the required resources. These tools have been used in libraries for many years, and they are used for organizing information resources in every library – big and small – in the world.

## Bibliographic formats

With the introduction of computers, librarians had to concentrate on building tools and techniques that would not only enable them to use computer technologies in processing information but would also help them share data about bibliographic items among libraries and institutions. Bibliographic formats define the way these records should be constructed. Bibliographic formats like MARC (MAchine-Readable Cataloguing), which gave rise to today's MARC 21 standard (discussed in Chapter 4), have been developed to store and process various data regarding information resources in online catalogues. Thus, classification, cataloguing and bibliographic formats together help libraries organize information resources, provide online access to those resources and share bibliographic data with other libraries. Details of bibliographic formats are discussed in Chapter 4.

We have seen that there are different approaches, tools and techniques for organizing and managing information resources in libraries. Various other tools and techniques are used for organizing information resources in other environments – such as in the database and web environments. Details of these are discussed in Chapter 2.

## Summary

In this chapter we have learned that classification is a natural human activity. Consciously or unconsciously, we classify things in order to find one or more things that share specific characteristics, in order to distinguish one thing from another. Bibliographic classification systems were developed to facilitate the organization of the bibliographic items on library shelves, so that related items can be kept together and unrelated items can be kept apart, with the overall intention of facilitating easy access to information resources. Cataloguing and subject indexing systems were developed to facilitate further information organization and access: they allow us to create specific records for each bibliographic item in a collection and organize them in a manner that allows users to find out which bibliographic items are available in a library and where they can be found. Thus, cataloguing and classification play very important and complementary roles. The former lets the user find out whether an item is available in the library, and the latter helps the user locate it on the shelf. Further details of classification and cataloguing tools and techniques appear in subsequent chapters.

## REVIEW QUESTIONS

**1** What is classification and what is its main purpose?

**2** What is bibliographic classification and what are the main objectives of a bibliographic classification system?

**3** What is cataloguing and what role does it play in the context of a library?

**4** What is a bibliographic format and what is the main role of a bibliographic format in the context of information organization and access?

**5** What is subject indexing and what role does it play in the context of information organization and access?

## References

Chowdhury, G. G. (2004a) *Introduction to Modern Information Retrieval*, 2nd edn, Facet Publishing.

Chowdhury, G. G. (2004b) Access and Usability Issues of Scholarly Electronic Publications. In Gorman, G. E. and Rowland, F. (eds), *Scholarly Publishing in an Electronic Era: International Yearbook of Library and Information Management 2004–2005*, Facet Publishing.

Corbett, E. V. (1966) *An Introduction to Librarianship*, 2nd edn, James Clarke and Co.

*Elsevier's Dictionary of Library Science, Information and Documentation* (1973) Elsevier Publishing Co.

Hanson, E. R. and Daily, J. E. (1970) Catalogs and Cataloguing. In Kent, A. and Lancour, H. (eds), *Encyclopedia of Library and Information Science*, Vol. 4, Marcel Dekker.

Hunter, E. J. (2002) *Classification Made Simple*, 2nd edn, Ashgate.

Hunter, E. J. and Bakewell, K.G. B. (1991) *Cataloguing*, 3rd edn, Library Association Publishing.

Maltby, A. (1975) *Sayers' Manual of Classification for Librarians*, 5th edn, André Deutsch.

*Oxford English Dictionary* (2006) www.oed.com/.

Prytherch, R. (comp.) (2005) *Harrod's Librarian's Glossary and Reference Book*, 10th edn, Ashgate.

Ranganathan, S. R. (1962) *Elements of Library Classification*, Asia Publishing House.

Svenonius, E. (2000) *The Intellectual Foundation of Information Organization*, MIT Press.

*Yahoo! Yellow Pages* (2006), http://yp.yahoo.com/.

# 2

# Information organization in non-library environments

## Introduction

Since the introduction of computers in information handling about five decades ago, a number of types of electronic information services have become part of the information landscape. These require new approaches to organizing information that are quite different in some cases from those used in conventional libraries. Information contained in online databases, and of late in web and digital libraries, requires different tools and techniques to organize it in a way that will facilitate better access. While specific tools and techniques for the indexing and retrieval of largely unstructured online information resources emerged over the last four decades or so, alternative techniques for handling structured data have more recently appeared in other areas of computerized information handling like DBMS (database management systems) and expert and knowledge-based information systems. This chapter provides a brief overview of the various approaches to organizing information in non-library environments. Specifically, it examines the traditional online database approaches, DBMS approaches and modern intranet and web-based approaches to organizing information. The basic differences between these various approaches to organizing information are discussed, and references are given to the appropriate chapters discussing various new techniques such as metadata, ontology, information architecture and the semantic web. Today's information professionals need to have an understanding of all the different approaches to organizing information in order to be prepared for every aspect of library and information management and services.

## Organization of electronic information

In the last chapter we discussed how classification schemes are used to assign class numbers to documents, which represent the subject contents of these documents and help us specify the locations of documents in a library's collection. However, for most users class numbers cannot be used to access items via catalogues, because they do not form part of the everyday vocabulary of the general users. In order to facilitate access to library catalogues, specific tools like subject heading lists were developed. Such tools specify natural language terms and phrases that can be assigned as subject headings or subject descriptors in catalogues and bibliographies.

With the introduction of computers in the late 1950s and early 1960s several databases of information resources – books, journals and conference papers, etc. – were developed. Such databases were produced by large libraries, like the National Library of Medicine in the US, or by commercial database producers. Online search service providers like Dialog emerged to provide access to online databases. These databases provide bibliographic details along with the abstracts, or sometimes the full text, of their information resources.

Online databases and search service providers use vocabulary control tools like thesauri to ensure standardization in the subject descriptors of information resources, and to facilitate information retrieval.

With the introduction of the web and digital libraries, the world of information has changed dramatically over the last decade in terms of volume, variety, format, nature and complexity of electronic information resources. This gave rise to the need for new and improved tools, techniques and standards for organizing information.

## The online database approach

Online information searches are conducted by means of a local computer that communicates with a remote computer system containing bibliographic and/or full-text databases (Chowdhury, 2004). Users can access the database(s) either directly through the database producer, or via an online search service provider (also called vendor).

While library classification schemes and subject heading lists have been used for organizing physical information resources in libraries, and for facilitating access to those resources, a different approach has been taken to organizing and providing access to information resources in online databases. The fundamental difference between the library and the online database approach is that in the latter case there are no physical items and we are not constrained by the requirements of physical location. In other words, for electronic resources we do not need to assign a class number for a physical location. In fact, in electronic databases information resources – say journal articles, conference papers or books – are arranged in computer memory in sequence, so each item has a specific memory location, which is used to access and retrieve it. But how would a user know where a required item has been stored? This is where the techniques of information retrieval come into play. In the simplest terms, the underlying processes of information retrieval are as follows.

1 Index terms (terms that describe the contents of the text) are extracted from each information resource in the collection – articles, books, etc. – and all index terms are arranged in an appropriate way to form an index file. This is called an inverted file. Each index term in the file is associated with a pointer (or multiple pointers) back to the relevant record (Chowdhury, 2004).
2 Computational procedures are developed to allow users to input search queries and thus search the index.
3 When user search terms match with those in the inverted index file, the corresponding pointers direct the user to the memory location(s) to retrieve the matched information resource(s) – bibliographic details and/or text.

How is this approach fundamentally different from the typical library approaches to organizing information?

1 In online databases an information resource occupies a specific memory location. In a library collection, the location mark is created on the basis of subject content, which facilitates organization of information resources based on their subject content. In a database the location mark (the memory location) has no relation to subject content; it is assigned by the computer system as the record is stored or a new record is created.
2 In both cases, users look for information resources using keywords or phrases. The only difference is that, in the traditional library, the subject representation, or the class number, is translated into verbal form by using a subject heading list; in a database there could be potentially many more subject terms – keywords and/or phrases – from every information resource, depending on the retrieval algorithm or the information retrieval model, which may or may not be controlled or expanded using appropriate tools like thesauri.

In essence, the fundamental difference is that unlike in the traditional library, in a database the location mark is not representative of the content of the items concerned, and no classification schemes are used to assign the location mark to the information resources. However, some information retrieval systems use automatic document classification systems based on document and index term similarity measures that facilitate access to information resources effectively and efficiently. These automatic classification systems are different from those of the traditional library approach in that they do not use a pre-designed classification scheme; rather, they use algorithms to compute document and term similarities (and differences) automatically to facilitate retrieval (Chowdhury, 2004; Salton, 1989; Salton and McGill, 1983).

## The DBMS approach

While online or electronic databases use some specific techniques and approaches, as discussed above, to organizing information resources to facilitate access to those resources, DBMS (database management systems) take a completely different approach. In essence, the database management approach aims to identify and store discrete data elements that represent the attributes (e.g. author, title, etc.) of each specific instance of an entity (i.e. a resource type, such as a book or an article) in a collection. A database may comprise one or more entities and each entity may have several attributes. The backbone of a database is the entity–relationship diagram that conceptually represents the various constituent entities, their attributes and, more importantly, their relationships.

The database management approach is similar to the online database or information retrieval approach, in that every constituent item is automatically assigned a memory location that has no relation whatsoever to its content or subject matter. The difference is that in case of online databases, users access information resources using keywords or phrases that form part of the constituent information resources, whereas in database management access is provided through the values representing specific attributes of the constituent items. That is to say, in a database management system a user can search by a range of values; for example it would be possible to retrieve details of all those employees in an organization who earn between £50,000 and £100,000. However, in a text retrieval system, a user may look for information by entering one or more keywords and the records that match those keywords are then retrieved; for example, it would be possible to retrieve all the records containing the phrase 'information retrieval'. It may be noted that, unlike online databases or information retrieval systems, database management systems were not designed to handle textual information resources. However, database management systems have been used in some cases to store and manage textual information.

Let's take a simple example in order to understand the difference between the two approaches. Suppose we created a database of journal articles using a database management system, and also an information retrieval system using the same collection of articles. In both cases, we can access articles by providing values for one or more key attributes such as the author name, title, and so on. The fundamental difference lies in the subject-based access. In a typical database management system each field can hold unique data, so the number of subject-related terms is potentially infinite. We may use a number of search terms or keywords in a given field, and use clever techniques for searching that field, but database management systems were basically not designed to handle text databases. They are not as efficient as information retrieval systems, which use specific techniques to process, organize and provide efficient access to a large collection of keywords or phrases that form the building blocks of the retrieval system. In other words, in a database management system one may enter more than one data element in a given field (e.g. one may enter house number, street name, place name, country name, etc. in a field designed to store addresses), but usually DBMS software is not designed to allow users to search by each data element (in this case the street name, house number, country, etc.) To put it in rather technical terms, DBMS software is not designed to handle repeatable fields, while this is exactly what text retrieval systems are designed to do – they allow us to store and search different data elements in a field in the form of subfields, or repeatable fields. DBMS technologies are outside the scope of this book; interested readers can find excellent introductions to DBMS in Hoffer, Prescott and McFadden (2006), Ramakrishnan and Gehrke (2002) and Riccardi (2003).

Despite these differences, database management systems, especially relational databases, have merits and have been used in organizing information in the library context, especially in cataloguing library resources. The FRBR (Functional Requirements of Bibliographic Records) model developed by IFLA (the International Federation of Library Associations and Institutions) uses the relational database model to create and represent relations between various bibliographic records in a collection. A relational database management system is a DBMS that stores data in the form of tables, where the rows represent database objects and columns represent the characteristics or attributes of those objects. The FRBR model is discussed in Chapter 3.

## The expert systems approach

Designers of expert systems have adopted a knowledge-based approach to organizing information. An expert system can be defined as a computer system that embodies knowledge about a specific problem domain, and can solve problems from the domain using its knowledge with a degree of expertise comparable to that of a human expert (Chowdhury, 2004).

Different kinds of knowledge are stored within the memory to be used by the program; this is called a knowledge base. The amount of knowledge required generally depends on the domain being handled (Chowdhury, 2004). There are various approaches to organizing information in a knowledge base.

Knowledge representation or semantic representation refers to representation created within the system from natural language statements (i.e. users can input queries in 'normal' language and so not need to format it or use symbols for it to be processed by the system). This internal representation is not limited to the language of the input text, and can be used for further processing; for instance, in matching user queries in information retrieval, in the creation of a database in one or more languages, and in any sort of text processing work. Several methods are used for knowledge representation, such as production systems, predicate calculus, semantic networks, case grammar, frames and conceptual dependency; while some of these knowledge organization and representation methods are quite simple, others are very complex (for details see Chowdhury, 2004).

The basic difference between knowledge-based approaches and information systems with text- or keyword-based information retrieval is that while the latter deals only with matching keywords or phrases, knowledge-based systems use syntax, semantics and context (pragmatics)-based approaches to information organization and retrieval. Expert systems and related technologies are outside the scope of this book; interested readers can find an useful introduction to expert systems in Chapter 19 of Chowdhury (2004).

## Organization of information on the internet

Information resources on the internet can be accessed in either of two ways if their location is not already known: by using a search engine or by browsing through a web directory. The first approach resembles the typical information retrieval approach, whereby an index file is created by extracting appropriate search keys from the webpages and then the index file is searched to locate the matching webpages. In the second approach a directory or a classification tree is created and then webpages are mapped onto the various 'branches' of the tree. The first approach has all the merits and weaknesses of online information retrieval, although the index and search algorithms and techniques are getting better every day and novel approaches are being introduced by web search engines. The second approach is resource-intensive as it involves the creation of a classification structure and then web pages have to be mapped on to the tree in accordance with their contents. Each method has its own merits and demerits but, overall, search engines have become more popular search tools on the web.

Some researchers have used library classification-based approaches to organize internet information resources, the notable examples being subject gateways like BUBL (www.bubl.ac.uk), Intute: science, engineering & technology (www.intute.ac.uk/sciences) and Intute: social sciences (www.intute.ac.uk/socialsciences). These use a library classification scheme or a vocabulary control tool to organize internet resources. Some systems like BUBL also allow users to access the collection through class numbers. Some search engines have used specialized programs to organize automatic classification and clusters of internet resources based on the keywords, links and other attributes of the webpages. Examples of such specialized search tools are Vivisimo (http://vivisimo.com/) and Kartoo (www.kartoo.com).

Libraries have long been creating summaries of bibliographic information resources that are used for resource discovery and information management; these are now called metadata. The most common example of metadata is the library catalogue. The term 'metadata' originated in the database world, and has become popular in the information world relatively recently in the context of electronic information resources (Haynes, 2004). Metadata plays a number of key roles ranging from resource discovery to information access and retrieval, sharing, processing, re-use and so on. Detailed discussions of metadata, metadata standards and metadata management appear in Chapter 8.

With the rapid growth of the web, several new approaches have been developed recently that allow users to organize a shared set of resources collaboratively by assigning classifiers, or tags, to each item. The practice is coming to be known by different terms like 'free tagging', 'open tagging', 'ethnoclassification', 'folksonomy' or 'faceted hierarchy', and is associated with popular online services such as furl (www.furl.net), del.icio.us (http://del.icio.us) or flickr (www.flickr.com) (ideant, 2004).

## New approaches to organizing information on intranets and the web

Most organizations now have to deal with information resources that reside on one or more institutional intranets, files, databases, spreadsheets or the web in general. Such information resources vary in form and format, and appropriate measures are required to organize them in order to facilitate easy access and retrieval. Several new tools and techniques, such as ontologies and information architecture, have been developed recently to organize and manage such information resources. Although the tools and techniques are new, their basic principles are the same as those used for organizing information in libraries and online database environments.

An ontology can be defined as a formal, explicit specification of a shared conceptualization. Gilchrist (2003) notes that Brian Vickery was one of the first in the LIS field to draw attention to the emergence of the term 'ontology' in knowledge engineering and information science. Two of the oldest and most widely known ontologies are WordNet (www.wordnet.com) and CYC (www.cyc.com). WordNet, a lexical tool, was developed by the Cognitive Science Laboratory at Stanford University, and contains some 100,000 word meanings organized in a taxonomy (Fellbaum, 1998). These are grouped into five categories – nouns, verbs, adjectives, adverbs and function words – and the meanings are related by synonymy, antonymy, hyponymy (the is-a relation), meronymy (part-of relationship between concepts) and morphological relations between word forms. WordNet is available free on the internet and has been used by a number of commercial organizations, including vendors of taxonomy software. The CYC ontology provides a foundation for common-sense reasoning. A large number of domain-specific ontologies have been built for applications such as machine translation, enterprise modelling, knowledge re-use and information retrieval. Overviews of some of these projects, and the tools used by them, can be found in Ding (2001), Ding and Foo (2002) and Fensel et al. (2003). Detailed discussions of ontology appear in Chapter 10.

Information resources on intranets and on the web are organized in a variety of ways. These differences arise because the organization is carried out by different people with different backgrounds and different perspectives. The area of study that deals with the organization, structuring and management of information on intranets and the web is called information architecture. This is a very broad definition, and does not cover all the purposes and functions of the concept of information architecture. Many different definitions of information architecture have been proposed (e.g. Dillon, 2005; Gilchrist and Mahon, 2004; Rosenfield and Morville, 2002; White, 2005). Basically, information architecture is concerned with organizing, labelling and managing a wide variety of information resources including those on intranets, the web and various computer systems in an organization. The basic idea behind information architecture is that the organization and management of a variety of information resources should be based on the specific context and requirements of a given organization and its different categories of users. Detailed discussions of information architecture appear in Chapter 11.

## The semantic web

Libraries have for a long time been using various tools and techniques for classification, cataloguing, resource sharing, etc. to achieve the broad objective of bringing related information resources together and helping users access information resources. Now, millions of information resources on the web are linked in a number of ways: through hyperlinks and through common keywords and phrases that are used to index and retrieve the resources. One way of accessing information on the web is based on the directory approach, which uses a pre-defined hierarchy of subjects and topics. The other way of accessing information is based on search engines that use crawlers to index webpages, and allow users to search for terms in large index files.

One of the major criticisms of the web has been that its information resources are not related or linked to each other based on their contents and meaning. It is a widely held view that the web can reach its full potential only if the data available on it can be accessed, processed and shared by automated tools globally. This is the vision of semantic web, a term coined by the creator of the web Tim Berners-Lee, whereby data on the web will be defined and linked in such a way that it can be used by machines not only for display purposes, but for the processing, integration and re-use of data across various applications (W3C, 2006). The semantic web, a collaborative effort led by W3C (the World Wide Web Consortium), provides 'a common framework that allows data to be shared and reused across application, enterprise, and community boundaries' (W3C, 2006). It is based on several new technologies like the RDF (resource description framework), URI (uniform resource identifiers), XML (extensible markup language) and ontologies. The concept of the semantic web and related technologies are discussed in Chapter 12.

## Summary

In this chapter we have provided a quick overview of the various non-library approaches to organizing information. Details of various new technologies for organizing and managing information on the internet, intranets and digital libraries, such as metadata, ontology, information architecture and the semantic web, appear later in this book. It should be noted that although the technologies, tools and approaches vary, the basic objective remains the same: to create an environment in which sem-antically related materials are kept in close proximity, and to provide easy access to those resources. Information professionals today should have a clear understanding of the different approaches to organizing information on a variety of different platforms – from the library shelf to the web.

## REVIEW QUESTIONS

1 How is information organized in online bibliographic databases?
2 What is the basic approach to organizing information in database management systems?
3 What is the basic approach to organizing information in expert systems?
4 What are the basic approaches to accessing information on the internet?
5 What is ethnoclassification?

# References

Chowdhury, G. G. (2004) *Introduction to Modern Information Retrieval*, 2nd edn, Facet Publishing.

Dillon, A. (2005) Pace, Timing and Rhythm in Information Architecture, *ASIS&T Bulletin*, **31** (2), www.asis.org/bulletin/dec-04/dillon.html.

Ding, Y. (2001) A Review of Ontologies with the Semantic Web in View, *Journal of Information Science*, **27** (6), 377–84.

Ding, Y. and Foo, S. (2002) Ontology Research and Development. Part I – a review of ontology generation, *Journal of Information Science*, **28** (2), 123–36.

Fellbaum, C. (ed.) (1998) *WordNet, an Electronic Lexical Database*, MIT Press.

Fensel, D., Hendler, J., Liberman, H. and Wahlster, W. (eds) (2003) *The Semantic Web*, MIT Press.

Gilchrist, A. (2003) Thesauri, Taxonomies and Ontologies – an etymological note, *Journal of Documentation*, **59** (1), 7–18.

Gilchrist, A. and Mahon, B. (eds) (2004) *Information Architecture: designing information environments for purpose*, Facet Publishing.

Haynes, D. (2004) *Metadata for Information Management and Retrieval*, Facet Publishing.

Hoffer, J., Prescott, M. and McFadden, F. (2006) *Modern Database Management*, 8th edn, Prentice Hall.

ideant (2004) *Bookmark, Classify and Share: a mini-ethnography of social practices in a distributed classification community. A del.icio.us study*, http://ideant.typepad.com/ideant/2004/12/a_delicious_stu.html.

Ramakrishnan, R. and Gehrke, J. (2002) *Database Management Systems*, 3rd edn, McGraw-Hill.

Riccardi, G. (2003) *Database Management: with website development applications*, Addison Wesley.

Rosenfield, L. and Morville, P. (2002) *Information Architecture for the World Wide Web*, 2nd edn, O'Reilly and Associates.

Salton, G. (1989) *Automatic Text Processing: the transformation, analysis, and retrieval of information by computer*, Addison Wesley.

Salton, G. and McGill, M. J. (1983) *Introduction to Modern Information Retrieval*, McGraw-Hill.

W3C (2006) *Semantic Web*, www.w3.org/2001/sw/.

White, M. (2005) *The Content Management Handbook*, Facet Publishing.

# 3
# Cataloguing

## Introduction

Cataloguing is one of the oldest information organization activities and has a history that is over 2000 years old. However, the history of modern-day approaches to cataloguing by using standard principles and practices is only a few hundred years old, and the most recent developments took place only over the past few decades. Modern day cataloguing activities are controlled by standard tools and guidelines, and virtually *de facto* standards like the *Anglo-American Cataloguing Rules* (AACR2 for short, referring to the second edition) exist; these need to be followed closely when preparing the entries for a catalogue of information resources, not only to make it easy to use, but to ensure that the entries are designed in a standard way, thus making it possible to share and exchange cataloguing data among various institutions. The basic concept of a library catalogue, and the various tools and techniques used in the cataloguing of bibliographic resources, are discussed in this chapter, and the process of cataloguing according to AACR2 is outlined. The implications of certain AACR2 guidelines on today's OPACs are also explored, as are the issues and techniques of cataloguing internet resources. The chapter also provides a brief description of the characteristics of the FRBR model.

## A brief history of library catalogues

Researchers have found evidence of some form of cataloguing of the records held in the library of Alexandria in ancient Egypt around 300 BC (Hanson and Daily, 1970). However, as far as modern cataloguing and its objectives and principles are concerned, history goes back just over two centuries. The first catalogue code at the national level was the French Code of 1791 (Hunter and Bakewell, 1991). In Britain, cataloguing rules were developed by Sir Anthony Panizzi for the British Museum library during the first half of the 19th century, and they were published in 1841

(Blake, 2002). However, it was Cutter who first specified the objectives of a library catalogue or a bibliographic system in 1876 (Cutter, 1904). These objectives were subsequently modified by Lubetzky; they were accepted internationally at a conference on cataloguing principles held in Paris in 1961, and are thus known as the ICCP Paris Principles. In 1997 these principles were again modified, this time under the auspices of the International Federation of Library Associations (IFLA), now called the International Federation of Library Associations and Institutions, with a view to modernizing the wording to suit electronic resources and rationalizing current bibliographic practice (Svenonius, 2000).

Catalogue codes have been devised to provide guidelines for preparing library catalogues to meet the objectives of cataloguing. Many new catalogue codes appeared in the early part of the 20th century: the *Anglo American Code* (AA) appeared in 1908, followed by the *Classified Catalogue Code* (CCC) of Ranganathan in 1934, the ALA code in 1949, the first edition of the *Anglo-American Cataloguing Rules* (AACR1) in 1967 and the second edition of the *Anglo-American Cataloguing Rules* (AACR2) in 1978. The latest revision of AACR2 was made in 2002, with an update in 2005.

## What is a library catalogue?

*Harrod's Librarian's Glossary* (Prytherch, 2005, 114) defines a catalogue as 'a list of book, maps and other items, arranged in some definite order. It records, describes and indexes (usually completely) the resources of a collection, a library or a group of libraries.' A library catalogue is an organized set of records of bibliographic information resources.

We prepare catalogues of resources in order to let users know what is in a collection. Over a century ago, Cutter (1904) specified the role of a library catalogue. A catalogue should:

■ enable a person to find a book by author, title and/or subject
■ show what the library has by a given author, on a given subject and in a given literature
■ assist in the choice of a book as to its edition and its character.

Cutter's principles, subsequently modified and adopted as the Paris Principles in 1961, specify three functions of a library catalogue:

identification, collocation and evaluation. They suggest that a catalogue should help the readers ascertain (Svenonius, 2000; Taylor, 2004a, 2004b):

- whether a library contains a book by a given author and title, or of a particular title where no author is specified, using a suitable substitute of title, if the author and title are inappropriate or insufficient
- which works the library has by a particular author
- which edition(s) of a particular work the library has.

It should be noted that nothing about subject access is mentioned here. In 1997, the objectives of a catalogue were reformulated by an IFLA study group to suit automated cataloguing environments, and to suit a variety of information resources not necessarily limited to books. Four major functions of a library catalogue were identified by the IFLA study group (IFLA, 1998; Svenonius, 2000):

- to find entities that correspond to the user's search criteria
- to identify an entity
- to select an entity that is appropriate to the user's needs
- to obtain access to (or, in other words, retrieve) the entity.

Catalogue records serve as a retrieval aid. In other words, catalogues allow users to obtain access to what they want to see in a collection, through the use of various search keys. Once a catalogue record is found, the descriptive part of the record enables the user to gather more information about the information resource, which helps the user make a decision about whether or not the item is useful.

In order for this to happen, we need to create an appropriate catalogue record for every item in a collection. Moreover, every catalogue record should be searchable by various search keys. This leads us to a number of questions, such as:

- How do we create catalogue records for different types of bibliographic items including audio and video records, computer files, etc.?
- What descriptive data elements should be recorded in a catalogue entry?
- What should be the various access points or search keys?
- In which order should the data elements appear?

Catalogue codes like the *Anglo-American Cataloguing Rules*, 2nd edition (AACR2), are used in libraries for this purpose.

## AACR2

In order to help librarians identify which data elements are required to denote a document, and how to represent them consistently (their sequence, punctuation, indentation, capitalization, etc.), several catalogue codes have been developed. The first edition of the *Anglo-American Cataloguing Rules* (AACR1) appeared in 1967, the second edition (AACR2) in 1978; a revised edition of AACR2 was published in 1988, a subsequent revision was made in 2002 and a 2005 update is now available (AACR2 Products, 2006; *Anglo-American Cataloguing Rules*, 2005).

AACR2 allows for up to eight areas in each catalogue entry, each area containing specific information about the document concerned, as shown below:

- area 1: title; other title information and statement of responsibility; subsequent statements of responsibility
- area 2: edition
- area 3: material (or type of publication) specific details
- area 4: publication, distribution, etc.
- area 5: physical description
- area 6: series
- area 7: notes
- area 8: standard number and terms of availability.

Figure 3.1 shows a typical catalogue record for a book.

## The process of cataloguing

Cataloguing involves four different, but interdependent, processes:

1 Description of the information resource: at this stage information is gathered about the information resource. It varies from one kind of information resource to another, but one mainly aims to gather information on the eight different areas mentioned above. The chief source of information for an information resource is to be found in

| System number | 007730907 |
|---|---|
| Author - personal | Chowdhury, G. G.  (Gobinda G.) |
| Title | Introduction to modern information retrieval / G. G. Chowdhury. |
| Edition | 2nd ed. |
| Publisher/year | London :  Facet,  2004. |
| Physical descr. | xii, 474 p. :  ill. ;  24 cm. |
| General note | Previous ed.: London: Library Association Publishing, 1999. |
| Bibliography etc. | Includes bibliographical references and index. |
| Subject | Information storage and retrieval systems. |
|  | Information organization. |
| Holdings (All) | Details |
| Shelfmark | m04/12689 DSC  Request |
| Shelfmark | HUR 025.04 Open Access  Request |
| Shelfmark | YK.2005.a.12763  Request |
| ISBN | 1856044807 (pbk.) :  No price |
| Dewey class. no. | 025.04  22 |

**Figure 3.1** A typical catalogue entry

the item itself, for example the title page (and the verso of the title page) of a book.

2 Choice of access points: at this stage the cataloguer has to decide the various points (e.g. author, title, etc.) that the user may use to access the information resource.

3 Choice of headings: at this stage the cataloguer has to decide the format for the headings. This is done to ensure standardization, and the cataloguer has to decide on various issues, such as: whether to use the heading in its natural order or in a reverse order, which one to use among the variant names (if any), whether to use the singular or the plural form and so on.

**4** References: at this stage the cataloguer provides links to various other access points that are deemed to be useful for users to access the same information resource.

The code provides specific rules for each activity involved in the process of cataloguing, as shown in Figure 3.2. AACR2 is divided into two parts. In Part 1, Chapters 1–12 provide specific cataloguing rules for specific types of information resources, and Chapter 13 provides guidelines for analysis. In Part 2, Chapters 21–26 consist of rules for determining access points in catalogues. These chapters also provide the rules for the form to be used for personal names, corporate bodies, geographic names and uniform titles, and tell us when to make references from one form of name or title to another form.

## Subject access to catalogues

As discussed above, catalogue codes like AACR2 provide guidelines for describing bibliographic items in catalogue records, for choosing access points and the form of entries, for choosing reference entries, etc. With regard to access points, AACR2 provides guidelines for choosing access keys that are provided in the documents themselves, such as author name(s), title, conference title, publisher name, conference title, etc. However, catalogue codes do not provide guidelines for assigning subject access points. Libraries use a different type of tool – called subject heading lists – for this purpose (see the subject headings in Figure 3.1). Subject heading lists provide specific guidelines for assigning subject headings to bibliographic records. They will be discussed in detail in Chapter 6.

## Implications of basic cataloguing rules for OPACs

OPACs are the interfaces that help users communicate with the collection(s) of a library. Typically, OPACs allow users to search the library's catalogue; they also provide some other facilities, such as checking borrower records, reserving reading materials, reading library news bulletins and so on (Chowdhury and Chowdhury, 2001). Although OPACs made their appearance in the mid-1970s, it was only at the beginning of the next decade that a significant number of libraries

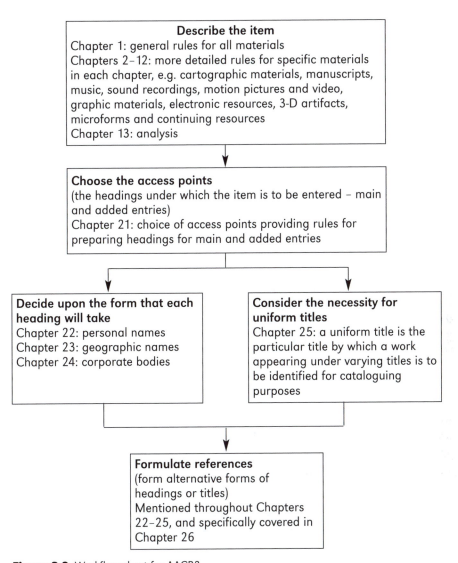

**Describe the item**
Chapter 1: general rules for all materials
Chapters 2–12: more detailed rules for specific materials
in each chapter, e.g. cartographic materials, manuscripts,
music, sound recordings, motion pictures and video,
graphic materials, electronic resources, 3-D artifacts,
microforms and continuing resources
Chapter 13: analysis

**Choose the access points**
(the headings under which the item is to be entered – main
and added entries)
Chapter 21: choice of access points providing rules for
preparing headings for main and added entries

**Decide upon the form that each
heading will take**
Chapter 22: personal names
Chapter 23: geographic names
Chapter 24: corporate bodies

**Consider the necessity for
uniform titles**
Chapter 25: a uniform title is the
particular title by which a work
appearing under varying titles is to
be identified for cataloguing
purposes

**Formulate references**
(form alternative forms of
headings or titles)
Mentioned throughout Chapters
22–25, and specifically covered in
Chapter 26

**Figure 3.2** Workflow chart for AACR2

switched from card catalogues to automated catalogues (Large and
Behesti, 1997). Those first catalogues were usually modules linked to an
automated circulation system, and had brief catalogue records and very
limited functionality. OPACs have improved significantly since then.
OPAC development can be classified into three distinct generations
(Hildreth, 1998; Rasmussen, 1999):

1 First generation: OPACs at the beginning were searchable typically by author, title and control number. Each record contained short and often non-standard bibliographic records.
2 Second generation: search functionality increased during this period to include access by subject headings, Boolean search capabilities, and browsing facilities. At this stage users could choose from more than one display format, and some OPACs developed different interfaces for novice and expert users.
3 Third generation: some of the problems and confusions of second-generation OPACs, such as lack of assistance, non-availability of integrated vocabulary control tools, etc. were overcome in the third generation. Third-generation OPACs incorporate features that are characterized by the facilities of the world wide web.

So, what are the implications of the cataloguing rules for OPACs? Although catalogue codes were originally devised for manual cataloguing, they are now used in the environment of automated cataloguing.

In the context of OPACs the concept of main and added entries does not apply, although catalogue codes prefer to maintain the distinction. According to AACR2, a main entry is a catalogue entry that is prepared under the main access point and contains the full catalogue description of a record; AACR2 prescribes one main entry for every record. However, there may be several added entries; an added entry is prepared under each additional access point with a minimum description of the record, and a reference to the main entry record.

In OPAC databases a user can search using one or more search parameters (author, title, keywords, ISBN, etc.) and the complete catalogue entry may be displayed as the search result. Initially, the cataloguing rules proposed three different levels of cataloguing (level one with the minimum details that would be useful to readers in smaller libraries, level two with adequate details that would be useful to readers in most libraries, and level three with every possible detail for readers in complex libraries). This was to help cataloguers in a manual cataloguing environment: catalogue entries were prepared on cards and hence there was a restriction on the amount of space available. The other reason for using lower levels of cataloguing was to save human resources. Cataloguers were advised to determine the level of information required by their potential users and to choose the level of cata-loguing accordingly. This is no longer important in the context of

OPACs: card space is no longer an issue in electronic catalogues, and neither are human resources as each catalogue entry can be generated automatically by computer. However, this does not mean that every catalogue entry should have the same level of description. The amount of detail to be provided is determined primarily by user requirements.

Guidelines related to choice of access points are also of less importance in the context of OPACs. These rules were formulated to help cataloguers in a manual cataloguing environment keep access points to a minimum because of restrictions in terms of space and number of card catalogues, as well as the manual labour involved in preparing card catalogues with different headings, arranging them in an appropriate order, and so on. These restrictions do not apply to OPACs, since in the electronic cataloguing environment the cataloguer has only to specify the access points and cataloguing software can then make the appropriate indexes. Therefore the cataloguer can choose as many access points as required for a given record.

Modern-day OPACs also include internet resources, and the catalogue codes were not originally devised to deal with them. They have some unique characteristics. Hence cataloguing of internet resources has become an important issue.

## Cataloguing of internet resources

A variety of information resources are now available through libraries, and these resources need to be properly catalogued. However, given the sheer volume of information resources – printed and electronic – currently available, libraries have to prioritize items to be catalogued. Mitchell and Surratt (2005) comment that, for the purpose of cataloguing, libraries usually give priority to resources that they pay for, resources that are produced by their parent organization, and other resources that are of interest to local users.

Internet resources have some specific characteristics that call for specialized cataloguing rules. These characteristics include: rapid growth in the number of resources, their availability through various agencies, the ways in which they are made available (e.g. access to a large collection in one go through a licensing agreement instead of a gradual growth in number), and the need for regular management and maintenance due to their changing nature (such as their location and terms of availability, etc.).

Internet resources vary significantly in terms of content (text, numeric, audio, image video, etc.), file format, mode and terms of availability and so on. Hence, while some parts of the AACR2 code can be used to catalogue internet resources, some new rules and guidelines are required to help cataloguers. The OCLC (Online Computer Library Center) has produced a number of documents providing guidelines for the cataloguing of electronic resources (Weitz, 2006). These guidelines apply specifically to certain fixed field elements such as type of record, bibliographic level and type of file code. However, rules for the description of resources can be found in various chapters of AACR2 and can be applied to internet resources.

To prepare the first two parts of a catalogue record for an internet resource (e.g. title proper and statement of responsibility, and edition), the specific guidelines in Chapter 9 of AACR2 may be followed. However, determining the responsibility of an internet resource can often be a challenging task, since a particular web page may contain several pieces of information that are created or owned by different users. Similarly, the content of web pages changes continuously, and often the different versions are not marked specifically. Hence, determining the edition information is often a difficult job. Field 856 in MARC 21 (discussed in Chapter 4) is to be used for electronic location and access information to an electronic resource.

For the publication and distribution area of the catalogue, a formal statement denoting the publication details of an internet resource, such as place, publisher and date, has to be provided. The guidelines provided in Chapter 9 of AACR2 may be followed for this purpose. For an internet resource a physical description is not required, and hence this section does not appear in the catalogue. The series information section should contain specific information on the series, if any, and the AACR2 guidelines may be followed.

The notes section (field 500 in MARC 21; discussed in Chapter 4) contains all other information that cannot be provided in any earlier section of the catalogue record, and yet is deemed to be of relevance. Guidelines provided in AACR2, especially in Chapters 1, 9 and 12, may be followed to prepare an entry for the notes section.

## FRBR (Functional Requirements of Bibliographic Records)

Library catalogues are used in a number of ways; for example,

- to find one or more items from the library's collection by conducting a search with one or more search keys
- to identify one or more items with some specified features
- to confirm that the retrieved items correspond to those looked for
- to select or choose one or more items in accordance with their specified content, format, etc.
- to obtain or acquire one or more selected items.

In addition, users may want to obtain items related to other items in the collection. For example, they may want to find a novel or a Shakespeare play in print form, and at the same may want to find the audio and/or video version of the staged drama, or a movie version if available. The FRBR model, created under the auspices of IFLA, is designed to facilitate this through a library catalogue. It is a framework for relating the data elements in bibliographic records to the needs of the users of those records. It is based on the entity–relationship model, the conceptual model behind relational database management systems, in the sense that it identifies bibliographic entities, their attributes and the relationships between them, and maps these to user tasks (IFLANET, 2004). In the FRBR model, it is assumed that the universe of bibliographic documents consists of entities that are related to each other and can be described through data elements or attributes.

Entities can be categorized into three groups (IFLANET, 2004):

- Group 1: entities that are the products of intellectual and artistic endeavour, described in bibliographic records, such as:
  - work: a distinct intellectual or artistic creation
  - expression: the intellectual or artistic *realization of a work*
  - manifestation: the physical embodiment of an *expression of a work*
  - item: a single exemplar of a manifestation
- Group 2: entities that are responsible for the intellectual or artistic content, the physical production and dissemination, or custodianship of a work – a person or a corporate body
- Group 3: entities that serve as the subjects of intellectual or artistic endeavour – concept, object, event, place and any Group 1 or Group 2 entities.

## Entities and their relationships

Relationships among Group 1 entities are shown in Figure 3.3. It may be noted that a *work* may be realized through one or more than one *expression*, and hence the relationship is one-to-many (one is shown by one ➜ and many is shown by ➜➜). An *expression*, on the other hand, is the realization of only one *work*, and hence the relationship is one-to-one. An *expression* may be embodied in more than one *manifestation*, and likewise a *manifestation* may embody more than one *expression*; thus there is a many-to-many relationship between these two entities. A *manifestation*, in turn, may be exemplified by more than one *item*, but an item may exemplify only one *manifestation*; therefore the relationship between these entities is one-to-many and one-to-one.

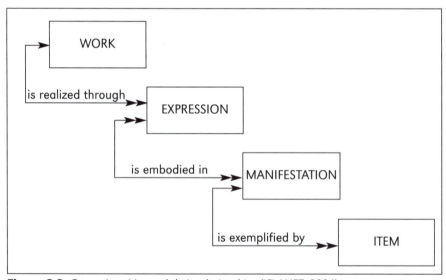

**Figure 3.3** Group 1 entities and their relationships (IFLANET, 2004)

The entities in the second group – individual people and corporate bodies – are those responsible for the intellectual or artistic content, the physical production and dissemination, or the custodianship of the entities in the first group. As shown in Figure 3.4, a *work* may be created by more than one *person* and/or more than one *corporate body*, and similarly a *person* or a *corporate body* may create more than one *work*; thus this is a many-to-many relationship. In the same way, an *expression* may be realized by more than one *person* and/or *corporate body*, and a *person* or *corporate body* may realize more than one *expression*; thus the relationship is *many-to-many*. Again, a *manifestation* may be produced by more than one *person* or *corporate body*, and a *person* or *corporate body* may produce more than one *manifestation; thus the relationship is many-to-many*. An *item* may be owned by more than one *person* and/or *corporate body*, and a *person* or *corporate body* may own more than one *item*; thus the relationship is *many-to-many*.

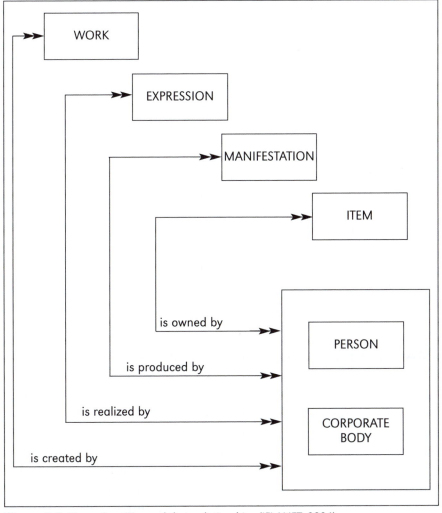

**Figure 3.4** Group 2 entities and their relationships (IFLANET, 2004)

The entities in the third group – *concept* (an abstract notion or idea), *object* (a material thing), *event* (an action or occurrence) and *place* (a location) – serve as the subjects of *works*. Figure 3.5 shows the relationships between entities in the third group and the *work* entity in the first group. It may be noted that a *work* may have as its subject more than one *concept*, *object*, *event* and/or *place*, and similarly a *concept*, *object*, *event* and/or *place* may be the subject of more than one *work*; thus the relationship is many-to-many. Figure 3.5 also shows the *subject* relationships between work and the entities in the first and second groups. It can be noted that a work may have as its subject more than one *work*, *expression*, *manifestation*, *item*, *person* and/or *corporate body*.

## Importance of the FRBR model

The FRBR model provides a framework for representing entities and their relationships within a catalogue. Examples of entities and their relationships are provided in the FRBR document (IFLANET, 2004). The FRBR model will enable a user to locate and link all the various manifestations and representations of a given work; for example, the FRBR model will enable a user to identify various instances of a specific work like Shakespeare's *Hamlet* – the printed version of the play in various languages, a CD or DVD version of the movie, various editions of the work and even various authors or corporate bodies that are related to it, such as movie producers, actors, translators, distributors etc. The FRBR model forms the basis for a revision of AACR2.

## RDA: Resource Description and Access

So, after AACR2 what's next? The answer is yes, there is will be further development - but with not quite the same name. The Joint Steering Committee responsible for revising AACR is working towards a thorough revision of AACR2 which (instead of producing AACR3) will give rise to a new standard called *RDA: Resource Description and Access*, scheduled for release in 2009, which will be published jointly by the American Library Association (ALA), Facet Publishing and their other international partners (Joint Steering Committee, 2007). Part A: Description of RDA will be based on the conceptual model of FRBR, and Part B: Access Point Control will be based on the FRAD (Functional

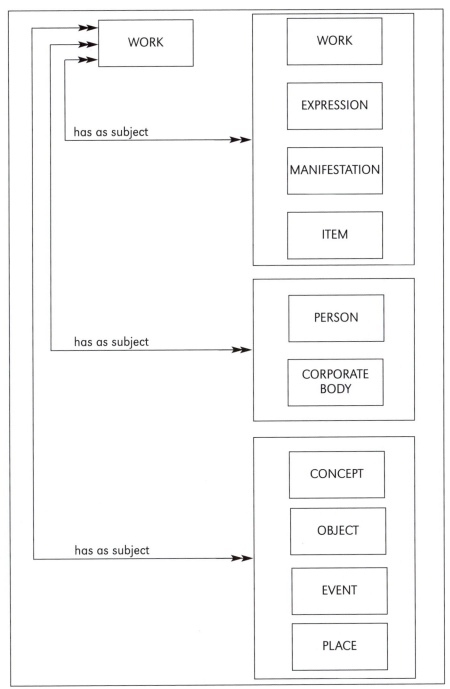

**Figure 3.5** Group 2 entities and 'responsibility' relationships (IFLANET, 2004)

Requirements for Authority Data). Further details of RDA and progress of work can be obtained online (Joint Steering Committee, 2007).

## Summary

In this chapter we have discussed the main objectives of library catalogues. AACR2, the *de facto* standard for cataloguing library resources, provides guidelines for the description of bibliographic items in catalogue entries. However, AACR2 does not provide specific guidelines for assigning subject headings to facilitate subject access to catalogues. For this, libraries use another set of tools called subject heading lists (discussed in Chapter 6).

Catalogue codes and bibliographic formats (discussed in Chapter 4) are used to create catalogue records and for computer handling of bibliographic data, including data transfer among various libraries and cataloguing agencies. Although these tools enable users to find, identify and locate the required bibliographic items, conventional library catalogues do not make appropriate provision for linking information resources that are related by subject, expression, manifestation, etc. An IFLA study group has developed a new model, called the FRBR framework, based on the entity–relationship model used in database management, which can be used to show the relationships among various components of catalogue records. It is expected that the new library catalogues based on this model will enable users to find and gather all related items through a catalogue.

Although some of the AACR2 guidelines, coupled with some specific features of bibliographic formats like MARC 21 (discussed in Chapter 4), can be used to catalogue internet resources, they are not adequate to handle every kind of internet resource. A new set of standards, called the metadata format (discussed in Chapter 8), are used for cataloguing internet resources. Nevertheless, cataloguing internet resources will remain a problem until the time every internet resource appears with an appropriate metadata set created either automatically or by the originator, and appropriate mechanisms/programs are available for the proper analysis, interpretation and use of these metadata elements to create a catalogue record for every resource. These issues are discussed in the later chapters of this book.

# REVIEW QUESTIONS

**1** What are the main objectives of a library catalogue?

**2** What is a catalogue code and why is it used?

**3** How applicable are the AACR2 rules and guidelines to the modern-day OPAC?

**4** How applicable are the AACR2 rules and guidelines to cataloguing internet resources?

**5** What is FRBR and what role is played by this model in the context of cataloguing?

# References

AACR2 Products (2006) *Anglo-American Cataloguing Rules Second Edition, 2002 Revision: 2005 update*, www.aacr2.org/uk/products_aacr2.html.

*Anglo-American Cataloguing Rules* (2005), 2nd edn, 2002 revision, 2005 update, Facet Publishing, American Library Association and Canadian Library Association.

Blake, V. L. (2002) Forging the Anglo-American Cataloging Alliance: descriptive cataloging, 1830–1908, *Cataloguing & Classification Quarterly*, **35** (1–2), 3–22.

Bowman, J. H. (2003) *Essential Cataloguing*, Facet Publishing.

Chowdhury, G. and Chowdhury, S. (2001) *Searching CD-ROM and Online Information Sources*, Library Association Publishing.

Cutter, C. A. (1904) *Rules for a Dictionary Catalog*, 4th edn, Government Printing Office (reprint, Library Association, 1962).

Hanson, E. R and Daily, J. E. (1970) Catalogs and Cataloguing. In Kent, A. and Lancour, H. (eds) *Encyclopedia of Library and Information Science*, Vol. 4, Marcel Dekker.

Haynes, D. (2004) *Metadata for Information Management and Retrieval*, Facet Publishing.

Hildreth, C. R. (1998) Online Library Catalogues as IR systems: what can we learn from research? In Yates-Mercer, P. A. (ed.), *Future Trends in Information Science and Technology*, Taylor Graham.

Hunter, E. J. and Bakewell, K. G. B. (1991) *Cataloguing*, 3rd edn, Library Association Publishing.

IFLA (1998) IFLA Study Group on the Functional Requirements for Bibliographic Records, *Functional Requirements for Bibliographic Records: final report*, K. G. Saur.

IFLANET (2004) *Functional Requirements for Bibliographic Records: final report*, www.ifla.org/VII/s13/frbr/frbr.pdf.

Joint Steering Committee for Revision of Anglo-American Cataloguing Rules (2007) *RDA: Resource Description and* Access, www.collectionscanada.ca/jsc/rda.html.

Large, A. and Behesti, J. (1997) OPACs: a research review, *Library and Information Science Research*, **19**, 111–33.

Mitchell, A. and Surratt, B. E. (2005) *Cataloguing and Organizing Digital Resources*, Facet Publishing.

Prytherch, R. (comp.) (2005) *Harrod's Librarian's Glossary and Reference Book*, 10th edn, Ashgate.

Rasmussen, E. (1999) Libraries and Bibliographical Systems. In Baeza-Yates, R. and Ribeiro-Neto, B. (eds), *Modern Information Retrieval*, ACM Press.

Svenonius, E. (2000) *The Intellectual Foundation of Information Organization*, MIT Press.

Taylor, A. G. (2004a) *The Organization of Information*, 2nd edn, Libraries Unlimited.

Taylor, A. G. (2004b) *Wynar's Introduction to Cataloguing and Classification*, 9th edn, Libraries Unlimited.

Weitz, J. (2006) *Cataloging Electronic Resources: OCLC-MARC coding guidelines*, www.oclc.org/support/documentation/worldcat/cataloging/electronicresources/default.htm.

# 4
# Bibliographic formats: MARC 21 and others

## Introduction

A library catalogue holds one or more record for every bibliographic item in order to facilitate access to the library's collection. But how are bibliographic records created and processed in order to generate these catalogue entries? In other words, how would a computer program recognize the different components of a bibliographic record and process them appropriately? There are two sets of problems here: first, we need to decide which data elements to store, and then we should decide how each data element is to be processed. Bibliographic data formats facilitate the creation, management and exchange of bibliographic data by prescribing the various data elements necessary to describe a bibliographic item, and also by providing guidelines for the processing of data stored for each data element. Over the years several bibliographic data formats have been created, and these all conform to the international standard ISO 2709: Format for Bibliographic Information Interchange. Of these, MARC is the most common – MARC 21 is the most widely used format in the world. This chapter begins with a discussion of the nature and characteristics of bibliographic formats, followed by a description of the structure of bibliographic data interchange format as given in the international standard ISO 2709. It then goes on to outline the various components and features of MARC 21, and of two other bibliographic formats that are used in different parts of the world – UNIMARC (UNIversal MARC) and CCF (common communications format).

## Bibliographic formats

A bibliographic format is a standard format that prescribes the various data elements to be used to create a record for a bibliographic item. Thus it governs the process of record creation and exchange (Chowdhury, 1996). A bibliographic format standardizes the creation of bibliographic records in a way that facilitates search and retrieval, both locally and through electronic networks, and the exchange of bibliographic information among libraries/information centres. Records created in a standard bibliographic format have three components (Gredley and Hopkinson, 1990; UBCIM, 1989), namely:

1 *Physical structure*: there are well-defined rules for the arrangement of data a computer storage medium. This may be considered as a container or carrier into which data may be placed. The carrier remains constant, although the data change from record to record.
2 *Content designators*: codes are used to identify the different data elements in the record (e.g. author, title, scale of map, starting date of a journal, etc.).
3 *Content*: the contents of a bibliographic record, governed by rules for the formulation of different data elements, are very closely tied up with content designators. Data elements have to be defined not only in terms of content but also in form, if the records are to be suitable for use by another agency.

The physical structure of bibliographic records is governed by ISO 2709 (1996). ISO 2709 was created for the exchange of bibliographic data on magnetic tape; it is now also being used for the formatting of bibliographic data sent online and stored on other media such as floppy disks and CD-ROMs.

Content designators are represented in most bibliographic formats by tags, indicators and subfield codes – in short, codes that define the different elements in the record. There are several bibliographic formatting schemes, such as MARC (MAchine-Readable Catalogue) and its family, and all use different systems of tags and other identifiers.

The form and content of data elements vary according to the cataloging principle and tool used. All bibliographic information systems need to follow some cataloguing rules in order to ensure consistency in data presentation – in display as well as in printed output.

Within an information system, the records that form the database will usually exist in a number of separate but highly compatible formats. Typically there will be (Simmons and Hopkinson, 1992):

- a format in which records will be input to the system
- a format best suited to long-term storage

■ a format to facilitate retrieval
■ a format (more often several formats) in which records will be displayed.

In addition, if organizations wish to exchange records, it will be necessary for each of these organizations to agree on a common standard. This is true of any network of organizations. Each must be able to convert to an exchange-format record from an internal-format record, and vice versa. If in any network of organizations, whether national or international, there is a single standard exchange format, information interchange within the network will be greatly facilitated, both technically and economically. However, there are many national standard exchange formats, and although there is a great deal of similarity among these formats, they are not identical and therefore records in different formats cannot be exchanged directly.

In order to resolve the lack of uniformity among national standard formats, international standard exchange formats have been developed. Within the community of national libraries the UNIMARC (UNIversal MARC) format was developed to provide a common format for exchange purposes. On the other hand, the community of abstracting and indexing services is served by UNISIST (the United Nations Internationational Scientific Information System), which uses its own set of content designators (Dierickx and Hopkinson, 1981). Both of these formats were designed to serve a limited range of institutions, and therefore it has not been possible to mix in a single record the bibliographic files from different types of organizations and services; consequently, an organization receiving records from various agencies needs a computer program to handle each type of record.

## ISO 2709: Format for Bibliographic Information Interchange

ISO 2709 is an international standard that specifies the requirements for a generalized machine format to hold bibliographic records. It should be noted that this standard does not define the content of individual records, or the meanings assigned to tags, indicators or identifiers; rather, it only prescribes a generalized structure that can be used to transmit records describing all forms of material capable of bibliographic description between data processing systems (ISO 2709, 1996).

According to ISO 2709, a bibliographic record should include the following fixed and variable-length fields:

**1** A record label: this is a fixed-length field holding basic information such as record length, record status, implementation codes (e.g. record type, bibliographic level, etc.), identifier length, etc.

**2** A directory: this is a variable-length field that holds the following information: a field tag (a three-character code for the field tag identifying the datafield); length of the field (a four-digit number showing how many characters are occupied by the datafield); and a five-digit number showing the starting character position of the field. The directory entry ends with a terminating symbol.

**3** A record identifier: this is a variable-length field containing characters that are uniquely associated with the given record, assigned by the agency preparing it.

**4** Reserved fields: these are variable-length fields used to hold reference data.

**5** Bibliographic data fields: these are variable-length fields holding the actual bibliographic data along with indicators.

**6** Field separators: each data field has to be terminated with a field separator.

**7** Record separator: each record has to be terminated with a separator symbol.

Below are examples of a label, directory and data field according to ISO 2709.

## Label

00101a_m__2200067___452_

The characters in the example label indicate the following, in sequence:

| | |
|---|---|
| 00101 | = total number of characters in the records |
| a | = record status (here it indicates that it is a new record) |
| _ | = blank space (one) |
| m | = bibliographic level: monograph |

| | |
|---|---|
| __ | = blank spaces (two) |
| 22 | = indication that the data in each field other than '001' begin with a two-character indicator and each subfield begins with a two-character identifier |
| 00067 | = length of the label and directory: the first character of the record is numbered 0, and therefore the label and the directory extend from character positions 0–66, and the data start at character position 67 |
| ___ | = blank spaces (three) |
| 452 | = indication that the second, third and fourth elements of each entry in the directory consist of four, five and two characters respectively. The first element, i.e. the tag, always consists of three characters in any implementation of ISO 2709, and is therefore not indicated |
| _ | = blank space (one) |

Labels are always 24 characters long.

## Directory

For example:

001000700000★★200001000023★★300001600007★★#

The directory consists of an entry for each of the fields present in the record (three in this case). The characters in the example directory indicate the following (in sequence):

| | |
|---|---|
| 001 | = tag for the first field |
| 0007 | = length of the field |
| 00000 | = starting character position |
| ★★ | = occurrence of the field and the number of the segment containing the field (not used here) |
| 200 | = tag for the second field |
| 0010 | = length of the field |
| 00023 | = starting character position |
| ★★ | = occurrence of the field and the number of the segment containing the field (not used here) |

|       |                                                                 |
|-------|-----------------------------------------------------------------|
| 300   | = tag for the third field                                       |
| 0016  | = length of the field                                           |
| 00007 | = starting character position                                   |
| ★★    | = occurrence of the field and the number of the segment         |
|       | containing the field (here not used)                            |
| #     | = end of directory                                              |

The second item in each directory entry (indicating the field length) is four characters long, the third item (indicating the starting character position of the field) is five characters long and the fourth item (indicating the occurrence of the field and the number of the segment containing the field) is two characters long, as indicated in the label.

## Data field

For example:

A12345#00@AJones@BJohn#00@AFruit#%

The characters in the example data field indicate the following (in sequence):

|        |                       |
|--------|-----------------------|
| A12345 | = data                |
| #      | = field separator     |
| 00     | = indicator           |
| @A     | = subfield identifier |
| Jones  | = data                |
| @B     | = subfield identifier |
| John   | = data                |
| #      | = field separator     |
| 00     | = indicator           |
| @A     | = subfield identifier |
| Fruit  | = data                |
| #      | = field separator     |
| %      | = record separator    |

It should be noted that this data field contains the actual data for the three fields with tags 001, 200 and 300. It may be seen in the previous section that the first field has a tag 001 and the data is seven characters long, starting from character position 00000. The data along with the field separator (please note that the field separator and subfield identifiers and indicators are included in counting the number of characters in a data field) in the first field is indeed seven characters long (six characters for 'A12345' and the '#' sign). The second field in the record has a field tag 200 and is ten characters long, starting at character position 23. Thus the second block starts with '00' (indicator) and ends with '#' (field separator), and there are two subfields, one containing the data 'Jones' and the other 'John':

00@AJones@BJohn#

The third field in the record has a tag 300 and holds data 16 characters long, starting at character position 27. This is the third item in the data field (the first item is seven characters long, starting at character position 00000 and continuing up to 00006, and the second item is 16 characters long, starting at character position 00007 and continuing up to 00022), starting at character position 00023 and continuing up to 00032. The last character, at position 00033, is a record terminator.

Thus if we take a look at the complete entry the record will look something like this:

00101a_m__2200067___452_001000700000★★200001000023★★3000016000
07★★#A12345#00@AJones@BJohn#00@AFruit#%

## MARC format

MARC is an acronym for MAchine-Readable Catalogue or Cataloguing. This general description is somewhat misleading because it is neither a kind of catalogue nor a method of cataloguing. In fact, MARC provides guidelines for assigning labels to each part of a catalogue record so that it can be handled by computer. The MARC format was primarily designed for libraries; however, the concept has since been embraced by the wider information community as a convenient way of storing and exchanging bibliographic data. The original MARC format was developed in the USA (by the Library of Congress) in 1965–6, and since then a number of formats have appeared that have the following common characteristics:

1 They adhere to the ISO 2709 record structure, or its equivalent national standard.
2 They are usually national formats based in a national library or national bibliographic agency and are the designated communication formats for exchange of bibliographic records with other similar organizations.

USMARC, UKMARC and other national MARC formats have some differences in terms of content designations.

The Library of Congress and the National Library of Canada harmonized the USMARC and CANMARC formats into a single edition in early 1999 under a new name: MARC 21. The Network Development and MARC Standards Office at the Library of Congress, and the Standards and Support Office at the National Library of Canada, maintain the MARC 21 format. The British Library decided in 2001 to discontinue using the UK MARC and to adopt MARC 21 (Bowman, 2002). The features of the MARC 21 format are discussed below.

## MARC 21

*MARC 21 Specifications for Record Structure, Character Sets, and Exchange Media* describes the structure of MARC 21 records, the character repertoires and encodings used, and the formatting of records for exchange via electronic file transfer, diskettes, and magnetic tape' (MARC 21, 2004).

The MARC 21 format provides a set of codes and content designators, and guidelines for managing and formatting electronic records of information resources. Formats are defined as follows:

- the MARC 21 format for bibliographic data, which contains format specifications for the data needed to describe, retrieve and control various forms of bibliographic material including books, serials, computer files, maps, music, visual materials and mixed material
- the MARC 21 format for holdings data, which contains format specifications for encoding data elements pertinent to holdings and location information for all forms of material

- the MARC 21 format for authority data, which contains format specifications for encoding data elements relating to bibliographic records that may be subject to authority control
- the MARC 21 format for classification data, which contains format specifications for encoding the data elements related to classification numbers and associated captions.
- the MARC 21 format for community information, which provides format specifications for records containing information about events, programs, services, etc. so that this information can be integrated into the same OPAC as other record types.

In addition, there are:

- MARC code list for languages
- MARC code list for countries
- MARC code list for geographical areas
- MARC code list for organizations
- MARC code list for relators, sources and descriptive conventions.

A MARC 21 record contains fields comprising a three-digit tag, up to two single-digit indicators and one or more subfields. Fields can be repeatable (denoted as R), meaning that the whole field may be repeated, or non-repeatable (denoted as NR).

A field tag can denote two types of information:

- information about the type of material – its physical characteristics, specific bibliographic aspects, etc. – required to process the record
- information about the bibliographic data elements required for cataloguing such as author, title publisher, etc.).

The MARC 21 format for bibliographic data specifies various groups of data elements, as shown in Table 4.1 (overleaf).

**Table 4.1** Components of a MARC 21 record

| Field tags (xx stands for numeric values from 00 to 99) | Component description |
| --- | --- |
| 0xx | Control fields |
| 1xx | Main entries |
| 2xx | Titles, edition and imprint information, etc. |
| 3xx | Physical description |
| 4xx | Series statements |
| 5xx | Notes |
| 6xx | Subject access entries |
| 7xx | Added entries and linking fields |
| 8xx | Series added entries and holdings information |
| 9xx | Fields for local use |

## Control fields

These fields hold information on bibliographic control numbers (assigned by agencies to specifically identify a bibliographic entity) and coded information:

- control fields 001–006 contain control numbers and other control and coded information, for example, date and time of processing as well as type of material; each control field is identified by a field tag and contains either a single data element or a series of fixed-length data elements identified by relative character position
- control field 007 contains information about the item's physical characteristics
- control field 008 contains 40 character positions (00–39) that provide coded information about the record as a whole and about special bibliographic aspects of the item being catalogued
- number and code fields (01X–04X) contain control and linking numbers, standard numbers and codes that relate to the bibliographic item described in the record (these are used to identify a given resource and to link it with other resources in the collection; they include Library of Congress control number, ISBN, publisher number, CODEN, language code, etc.)

■ classification and call number fields (05X–08X) contain classification and call numbers related to the item described in the bibliographic record.

## Main entry fields (1XX)

This field stores information that is used to create the main entry heading of a bibliographic record. The following are main entry fields:

■ 100 – main entry – personal name (NR)
■ 110 – main entry – corporate name (NR)
■ 111 – main entry – meeting name (NR)
■ 130 – main entry – uniform title (NR).

For example, a work of Sir Winston Churchill will be entered as:

100 1#$aChurchill, Winston,$cSir,$d1874-1965

(where the subfield $a is used to denote personal name, $c denotes title and $d denotes associated dates such as dates of birth, death, etc.; 0, 1 and 3 are used as indicators (0 for forename, 1 for surname and 3 for family name; # is an undefined character).

## Title and title-related fields (20X–24X)

These fields store the title of the item and also information on variant titles, if applicable. Different codes are used for storing title information: 210 – abbreviated title, 222 – key title, 240 – uniform title, 245 – title statement, etc.

A typical MARC entry for the title of the journal *Library Review* will be as follows:

222 #0$a Library review

where 0 denotes that there is no non-filing character, and $a denotes that this is the key title of the journal.

## Edition, imprint, etc. field (250–270)

These fields store information regarding edition, imprint, publisher, address and other publication related information. Different tags are used for storing this information: 250 – edition statement, 256 – computer file characteristics, 260 – publication, distribution, etc.

A typical MARC entry for the edition statement of a book will be as follows:

250 ##$a2nd ed.

where the two # signs denote undefined indicators, and $a denotes that this is an edition statement.

It may be noted that field 256 holds important data about electronic records. A typical example of a field holding data for computer programs is:

256 ##$aComputer programs (2 files: 4500, 2000 bytes)

## Physical description, etc. fields (3XX)

These fields store information on the physical characteristics, publication frequency, price and physical arrangement of the item. Information about the dissemination of bibliographic items and the security status of bibliographic data relating to them is also recorded here. Different tags are used to store this information: 300 – physical description, 306 – playing time, 310 – current publication frequency (NR), 340 – physical medium, etc.

A typical MARC entry for the physical designation of a book and a computer file will be as follows:

300 ##$a345p. ;$c23cm.
300 ##$a1 computer disk :$bsd., col. ;$c3½ in.

where $a denotes the extent (e.g. pages, volume, etc.), $b denotes other physical details (such as colour, playing speed, etc.) and $c denotes the size.

## Series statement fields (4XX)

This field can be repeatable, to show that there may be more than one series. Fields 440 and 490 contain series statements. A typical MARC record holding a series statement is:

440 #0 $a Library and information science series $v no. 5

where $a denotes the title of the series and $v denotes the number of items in the series.

## Notes field (5XX)

There are various note fields: Part 1 (50X–53X) and Part 2 (53X–58X). A number of fields have been designated for storing different types of notes associated with different types of documents. A typical note field is:

500 ##$a Based on an Indian folk tale

where the two # signs denote undefined indicators.

## Subject access fields (6XX)

These are used to store information on subject headings, or other subject access terms that provide additional access to a bibliographic record. In all, 13 fields have been designed to store different types of subject access information: 600 is used to store subject added entry for personal names, 650 topical terms, 651 geographic names, and so on. The following is a typical example of a MARC record for a subject added entry field:

650 #0$aArchitecture, Modern$y20th century

where $a denotes topical term and $y denotes chronological subdivision.

## Added entry fields (70X–75X)

These fields contain information that is not provided through any of the following fields: main entry (1XX), subject access (6XX), series statement (4XX), series added entry (8XX) or title (20X–24X).

Linking entry fields (76X–78X) contain information that links related bibliographic items.

### Series added entry fields (8XX)

In addition to information on series added entries (i.e. an added entry containing the series information), these fields also hold information on location and are extremely useful for electronic records.

The series added entry fields (80X–830) contain a name/title or a title used as a series added entry when the series statement is contained in field 490 (series statement) or field 500 (general note) and a series added entry is required for the bibliographic record.

The holdings, location, alternate graphs, etc. fields (841–88X) contain descriptions of data elements which may appear either in bibliographic records or in separate MARC records. Field 856 is particularly important for electronic records, especially internet and web resources; this field contains the information needed to locate and access an electronic resource. A large number of subfield codes and indicators have been proposed for this field. The following is a typical example of information stored for a web page:

> 856  40$uwww.ref.oclc.org:2000$zAddress for accessing the journal using authorization number and password through OCLC FirstSearch Electronic Collections Online. Subscription to online journal required for access to abstracts and full text

where the first indicator 4 denotes that the item can be accessed through HTTP (hypertext transfer protocol), the second indicator 0 denotes that the electronic location in field 856 is for the same resource described by the record as a whole, $u denotes the URL (uniform resource locator, i.e. the address of a web page) and $z denotes a note.

Figure 4.1 shows the MARC 21 entry for the following book held at OCLC's WorldCat (www.oclc.org/worldcat/):

> Chowdhury, G. G. (Gobinda G.) Introduction to modern information retrieval / G.G. Chowdhury. 2nd edn London : Facet, 2004. xii, 474 p. : ill. ; 24 cm

## UNIMARC format

Several versions of the MARC format have emerged since the early 1970s – UKMARC, USMARC, CANMARC, etc. – whose paths diverged

```
010       2004380013
040       UKM $c UKM $d DLC $d NLGGC $d BAKER
015       GBA3V5710 $2 bnb
016  7    007730907 $2 UK
019       52784925 $a 56469507
020       1856044807 (pbk.)
029  1    NLGGC $b 257462287
029  1    UKM $b bA3V5710
050  00   ZA3075 $b .C47 2004
082  04   025.04 $2 22
084       06.64 $2 bcl
092       $b
049       UKGA
100  1    Chowdhury, G. G. $q (Gobinda G.)
245  10   Introduction to modern information retrieval / $c G.G. Chowdhury.
250       2nd ed.
260       London : $b Facet, $c 2004.
300       xii, 474 p. : $b ill. ; $c 24 cm.
500       Previous ed.: London: Library Association Publications, 1999.
504       Includes bibliographical references and index.
650   0   Information storage and retrieval systems.
650   0   Information organization.
650  17   Information retrieval-system en. $2 gtt
650  17   Information storage and retrieval. $2 gtt
938       Baker & Taylor $b BKTY $c 89.95 $d 89.95 $i 1856044807 $n
0004423319 $s active
```

**Figure 4.1** An entry in MARC 21 format

owing to different national cataloguing practices and requirements. Differences in the data contents of these formats mean that editing is required before records can be exchanged. One solution to this incompatibility was to develop an international (universal) MARC format that would accept records created in any MARC format: records in one MARC format could be converted into UNIMARC and then be converted into any other MARC format. This would require each national agency to write only two programs – one to convert to UNIMARC and another to convert from UNIMARC – instead of having to write a separate program for each MARC format.

In 1977 IFLA brought out the UNIMARC format. Its primary purpose was to facilitate the international exchange of data in machine-readable form between national bibliographic agencies (*UNIMARC Manual*, 1994). This was followed by a second edition in 1980 and a UNIMARC handbook in 1983. All these focused primarily on the cataloguing of monographs and serials, and incorporated the international progress made towards the standardization of bibliographic information reflected in the International Standard Bibliographic Description (ISBD; see ISBD(G), 1977). The latest edition of the *UNIMARC Manual* (2nd edition) was published in 1994. Details of the UNIMARC, including updates, are available on the web (IFLANET, 1999).

This list from the IFLANET website (1999) outlines what a field in a UNIMARC record should contain:

- Tag: a three digit number, e.g. 700, which defines the type of bibliographic data.
- Indicators: two single digit numbers right after the tag, eg 700#0, that either refine the field definition or show how the field should be treated for catalogue production, e.g. by signaling that a note should be made; blanks are shown by the hash sign # to distinguish them from a space.
- Within each field, data is coded into one or more subfields, e.g. 700#0$a ... $b ..., etc., according to the kind or function of the information. The effect of the subfield coding is to refine further the definition of the data for computer processing. The subfield identifiers consist of a special character, represented by a $ in the examples, and a lower case alphabetic character or a number 0–9.
- Each field is followed by an end of field mark represented by the 'at' sign @ in the examples.

UNIMARC consists of the following blocks (IFLANET, 1999).


## Identification block

0XX is the identification block, which stores the information needed to identify the record, such as

001 0192122622@

(where the field holds an identification number), or

010##$a0-19-212262-2$d£12.95@

(where the field holds the ISBN, $a, and price, $d).


## Coded information block

1XX is the coded information block. Field 100 stores general processing data; 101 stores language information. For example:

    1011#$aeng$cfre@

gives details of the languages involved, the value of the first indicator (1) shows that the item is a translation. It is a translation into English ($a) from French ($c).

## Descriptive information block

2XX stores information that describes the item, such as title and statement of responsibility. For example:

    2001#$a{NSB}The {NSE}lost domain$fAlain-Fournier$gtranslated from the French by Frank Davison$gafterword by John Fowles$gillustrated by Ian Beck@

Here the title field (200) has a first indicator (1), showing that the title is significant. In a browsable list – printed, microform or electronic - there would be an added entry filing at 'Lost domain'. To avoid listing the title file under 'T' in an alphabetical listing, 'The[space]' is preceded and succeeded by a special character (represented here by {NSB}and {NSE}) to show where non-sorting characters begin and end. These characters would not appear in any listing or on a reader's computer screen. $f indicates the first statement of responsibility; subsequent statements are coded $g.

Other fields in the 2XX series hold other specific items of information. For example, field 210 holds details about publication, distribution, etc.

    210##$aOxford$cOxford University Press$d1959@

Field 215 holds information about the physical description of the item:

    215##$aix,298p,10 leaves of plates$cill, col.port$d23cm@

## Notes block

3XX stores specific notes. For example:

311##$aTranslation of: Le Grand Meaulnes. Paris : Emile-Paul, 1913@

pertains to linking fields (see field 454 below); this note is produced by the computer and has not been provided by the catalogue).

## Linking entry block

4XX holds information on a linked item. For example:

454#1$1001db140203$150010$a{NSB}Le {NSE}Grand Meaulnes$1700#0$a Alain-Fournier$f1886-1914$1210##$aParis$cEmile-Paul$d1913@

This is a linking field pointing to the original as the present item is a translation. Each $1 subfield holds the contents of a field from the linked item; in this example it holds 001 record identifier, 500 uniform title, 700 author and 210 publication details

## Related title block

5XX contains information regarding a related title, a uniform title, etc. For example:

50010$a{NSB}Le {NSE}Grand Meaulnes$mEnglish@

denotes a uniform title. The first indicator serves the same function as the 200 field. The $m (language) subfield allows the catalogue to group together all English translations of this work.

## Subject analysis block

6XX is the subject analysis block. For example:

676##$a843/.912$v19@

This field holds a DDC number from the 19th edition of DDC (denoted by $v). The '/' is a 'prime mark': libraries that do not have many items in French literature could drop it and everything beyond it, giving a class number of '843' for French literature.

680##$aPQ2611.O85@

denotes the Library of Congress class number.

## Intellectual responsibility block

7XX stores information about intellectual responsibility. For example:

700#0$aAlain-Fournier,$f1886-1914@

This field stores information on the person primarily responsible for the work; the second indicator is 0 as this is a name entered under forename rather than under surname; the $f subfield holds the author's dates of birth and death. For a second statement of responsibility, we may enter

702#1$aDavison,$bFrank@

where the second indicator is 1, as this is a name entered under surname; the forename is in the $b subfield.

## International use block

An example of the use of the 8XX block is:

801#0$aGB$bWE/N0A$c19590202$gAACR2@

This field holds information on the 'originating source', and is especially useful for a union catalogue. Here, subfield $a holds the code for the country and $b the code for the agency creating the record; $c is the date of creation and $g holds details of the cataloguing code used – in this case AACR2.

## National use block

9XX, national use block, holds information for local use. For example:

98700$aNov.1959/209@

stores the shelfmark.

UNIMARC is maintained by a permanent committee, called the Permanent UNIMRC Committee, or PUC in short, formed in 1991 under the aegis of IFLA. The UNIMARC Forum website (www. unimarc.net) provides information on UNIMARC activities.

## CCF

The CCF (common communications format) was developed in order to facilitate the exchange of bibliographic data between organizations. It was first published by UNESCO in 1984 and then updated in 1988 and 1992 (Simmons and Hopkinson, 1992). CCF was designed to follow the following basic principles:

- The structure of the format conforms to the international standard ISO 2709.
- The core record consists of a small number of mandatory data elements essential to bibliographic description.
- The mandatory elements are augmented by some optional data elements.
- A standard technique is used to accommodate bibliographic levels, relationships and links between bibliographic entities.

A second edition of CCF was published in 1988, and subsequently it was decided that the scope of CCF would be extended to incorporate provisions for data elements that record factual information and are frequently used for referral purposes. As a result, the third edition of CCF was divided into two volumes: CCF/B for holding bibliographic information and CCF/F for factual information. CCF (B and F, taken together) has been designed to provide a standard format for three major purposes (Simmons and Hopkinson, 1992):

- to permit the exchange of records between information agencies, including libraries, abstracting and indexing services, referral systems and other kinds of information agencies
- to permit the use of a single set of computer programs to manipulate records received from various information agencies regardless of their internal record-creation practices

■ to serve as the basis of a format for an agency's own bibliographic or factual database by providing a list of useful data elements.

The data elements specified in CCF for recording bibliographic and factual information in databases are presented in Figure 4.2.

CCF makes provision for holding in one (integrated) database system a number of different kinds of records: records of books, periodicals, reports, theses, cartographic materials, patents and standards, as well as profiles of projects, institutions and people.

| | | | |
|---|---|---|---|
| 001 | Record identifier | 320 | Name of meeting |
| 010 | Record identifier for secondary segments | 330 | Affiliation |
| 011 | Alternative record identifier | 340 | Countries associated with parent |
| 015 | Bibliographic level of secondary segment | 400 | Place of publication and publisher |
| 020 | Source of record | 410 | Place of manufacture and manufacturer |
| 021 | Completeness of record | 420 | Place of distribution and distributor |
| 022 | Date entered on file | 430 | Address |
| 023 | Date and number of record version | 440 | Date of publication |
| 030 | Character sets used in record | 441 | Date of legal deposit |
| 031 | Language and script of record | 442 | Dates related to patent |
| 040 | Language of item/entity | 444 | Dates related to standard |
| 041 | Language and script of summary | 446 | Dates related to thesis |
| 050 | Physical medium | 448 | Start and end dates |
| 060 | Type of material | 450 | Serial numbering and date |
| 061 | Type of parent document | 460 | Physical description |
| 062 | Type of factual information | 465 | Price and binding |
| 063 | Type of standard | 470 | Mathematical data for cartographic material |
| 080 | Segment linking field: vertical relation | 480 | Series statement |
| 085 | Segment linking field: horizontal relation | 490 | Part statement |
| 086 | Field to field linking | 500 | Note |
| 088 | Record to record linking | 510 | Note on related items/entities |
| 100 | International Standard Book Number (ISBN) | 520 | Serial frequency note |
| 101 | International Standard Serial Number (ISSN) | 530 | Contents note |
| 102 | CODEN (for serials) | 600 | Abstract/description |
| 110 | National bibliography number | 610 | Classification scheme notation |
| 111 | Legal deposit number | 620 | Subject descriptor |
| 120 | Document number | 650 | Services provided |
| 125 | Project number | 700 | Human resources |
| 130 | Contract number | 705 | Equipment and other resources |
| 200 | Title | 710 | Financial resources |
| 201 | Key title | 715 | Income components |
| 210 | Parallel title | 716 | Expenditure components |
| 230 | Other title | 800 | Nationality |
| 240 | Uniform title | 810 | Educational qualifications |
| 260 | Edition statement | 820 | Experience of person |
| 300 | Name of person | 860 | Project status |
| 310 | Name of corporate body | | |

**Figure 4.2** CCF (B and F)

Figure 4.3 shows a few lines from a CCF record. There are three components: the field tag comprising three digits, the segment identifier and the occurrence identifier; and also the data fields. A segment identifier is a single character that designates the data field as being a member of a particular segment; in this example all are denoted by '0', meaning that this is not part of any segment (because this is a monograph record). An occurrence identifier is a single character that specifies whether this is a single or a multiple occurrence of a data field with the same field tag; in the example, all are denoted by '0', meaning that each one is a single occurrence. A data field may be repeatable: more than one data element can be accommodated in a data field with a given tag – for example, in field 620 where more than one keyword is separated by field separator '@'.

```
001   0   0   A012345
020   0   0   00@APBPrivate
021   0   0   @AB
022   0   0   00A@A20060831
030   0   0   00@B2
040   0   0   00@Eng
060   0   0   00@A100
100   0   0   00@A0004423319
200   0   0   00@AIntroduction to modern information retrieval
300   0   0   00@AChowdhury@BG
400   0   0   00@ALondon@BFacet Publishing
440   0   0   00@A20040000@C1
460   0   0   00@Axii, 474p.
600   0   0   00@AThe book provides a detailed coverage of the
      field of information storage and retrieval. The first edition of the
      book was published in 1999
610   0   0   00@A025.04@CD
620   0   0   00@Ainformation organization@AInformation
      retrieval@AInformation storage and retrieval
```

**Figure 4.3** A simple CCF record

## Summary

Bibliographic formats play a key role in the creation, management and exchange of bibliographic records. They ensure standardization in the structure of bibliographic records, and they facilitate the exchange and sharing of data among various agencies. Although many bibliographic formats have been developed over the past few decades, MARC 21 is now the most widely used.

Standard bibliographic exchange formats like UNIMARC and CCF were developed in order to facilitate the exchange of bibliographic data among agencies using different bibliographic formats. These formats are used in the creation of bibliographic records in some agencies, especially in many developing countries.


## REVIEW QUESTIONS

**1** What is a bibliographic data format and what purpose does it serve in organizing information?

**2** What is ISO 2709 and what purpose does it serve in the context of information organization?

**3** What is MARC and what is it used for?

**4** What is MARC 21 and what role does a MARC 21 record play in organizing bibliographic information?

**5** What role is played by UNIMARC and CCF in the organization of bibliographic information?


## References

Bowman, J. H. (2002) *Essential Cataloguing*, Facet Publishing.

Chowdhury, G. G. (1996) Record Formats for Integrated Databases: a review and comparison, *Information Development*, **12** (4), 218–23.

Dierickx, H. and Hopkinson, A. (eds) (1981) *Reference Manual for Machine-readable Bibliographic Descriptions*, 2nd rev. edn, UNESCO.

Gredley, E. and Hopkinson, A. (1990) *Exchanging Bibliographic Data: MARC and other international formats*, Library Association Publishing.

IFLANET (1999) *Universal Bibliographic Control and International MARC Core Programme*, www.ifla.org/v1/3/p1996-1/unimarc.htm#.

ISBD(G)(1977) *ISBD(G): general international standard bibliographic description: annotated text*, IFLA International Office for UBC (Universal Bibliographic Control).

ISO 2709:1996 *Documentation: format for bibliographic information interchange on magnetic tape*, 3rd edn, International Organization for Standardization.

MARC 21 (2004) *MARC 21 Specifications for Record Structure, Character Sets, and Exchange Media*, Library of Congress, Network Development and MARC Standards Office, www.loc.gov/marc/specifications/spechome.html.

- assigning a shelf address, so that every document on the library's shelves has a specific location
- collocating items, whereby documents on the same or similar subjects are placed together on the library's shelves to enable users to find items on the same subject in one place within a library
- linking items: the catalogue record of an item to the item itself on the shelf; users look through the catalogue and once the items have been found, the corresponding call numbers can be used as references to locate items on the shelves
- providing browsing facilities, as the structure of a bibliographic classification can be used to browse a collection on the library's shelves or in an electronic collection.

Classification schemes were originally devised to classify bibliographic materials in libraries. However, subsequently the tools have been used for organizing and retrieving electronic information resources (e.g. CyberDewey, BUBL, etc. – discussed later in this chapter).

## Classification schemes

Bibliographic classification schemes are used to assign a class number to every bibliographic item in a collection, to represent its subject matter. Thus, ideally, a classification scheme should enable us to find an appropriate class number for every possible discipline and subject in the universe of knowledge. In order to make this happen, a classification scheme may take one of two broad approaches: either to enumerate all the possible subjects and topics in every discipline, each with a special number, or to make provision for building class numbers for every subject and topic by using specific rules of synthesis and techniques of classification. In either case, however, the basic objective remains the same: related subjects should be kept in close proximity while unrelated subjects should be kept apart.

Although, as discussed in the following sections, classification schemes differ in terms of approach, structure and principles, they all have three main components:

- a set of subjects, called main classes, and their subdivisions
- notations for every class and subclass
- an index.

The main part of a classification scheme, called the schedule or the main table, comprises the main classes and subclasses arranged by class mark or notation. The main schedule is supplemented by a number of smaller tables that are named differently in different classification schemes (tables, auxiliary tables, common isolates, etc.). The schedule and the tables are arranged by notation; hence, in order to facilitate access to specific class numbers or a given topic, classification schemes provide an index of all the topics listed in the schedule and tables, arranged alphabetically. The notations used in a classification scheme form its backbone; most classification schemes use a combination of Indo–Arabic numerals, letters and symbols.

## Notation

A notation is a symbol that is used to represent a subject or a class in a classification scheme. Notation can be of two types: pure notation uses only one type of symbol, and mixed notation uses more than one type of symbol. Most classification schemes use mixed notations that are a combination of Indo–Arabic numerals, alphabets and punctuation marks and other symbols.

The notations in a library classification scheme should possess a number of qualities, briefly discussed below.

### Expressiveness

Expressiveness is reflected in the structure of the classification scheme. In other words, an expressive notation scheme uses a highly systematic hierarchy of subject terms. Thus, users can understand the structure and can easily broaden a search (by going up a class number) or narrow it down (by going down). For example, in Dewey Decimal Classification (DDC):

610  Medicine and health
615  Pharmacology and therapeutics
615.8  Specific therapies and kinds of therapies
615.82  Physical therapies
615.822  Therapeutic massage
615.8222  Acupressure

However, one disadvantage of such expressiveness of notation is that the class number may become unnecessarily lengthy. Another disadvantage is that it may provide very little space to add new concepts, and therefore it could limit another quality of notation called hospitality, which is discussed later in this chapter.

## Mnemonics

A mnemonic notation is one which can be remembered easily. A mnemonic notation can use either numeric digits or letters, and can be one of two types: systematic mnemonic notation or literal mnemonic notation.

Systematic mnemonics use numerals, and the number is always the same for a concept, whatever the subject. For example, in DDC:

Dictionary of Medicine: 510.3
Dictionary of Religion: 200.3
'0.3' always stands for 'dictionary'.

English Drama: 812
French Drama: 842

The number '2' stands for 'drama' in the literature class.

In contrast, the letters of the alphabet are used in literal mnemonics. For example, in LC, G stands for geography and T for technology.

## Simplicity

Simplicity is a very desirable quality of notation which ensures that the class number is easy to grasp.

## Uniqueness

The notation used for every class should be unique, and therefore easily identified.

## Brevity

A short number is always easy to use/grasp, and notations should therefore be as brief as possible. However, a number of factors affect brevity, such as: the base of the notation, how the notation is allocated and the synthesis of a notation.

## Flexibility

This is a very important feature. In a flexible scheme, citation order can be altered according to user's preferences.

## Hospitality

In order for the classification scheme to grow over time, notation schemes should have provisions to accommodate new concepts or subjects whenever they appear. For example, in DDC:

300   Social sciences
310   Statistics
[311]   [Unassigned]
[312]   [Unassigned]
[313]   [Unassigned]
314–319   General statistics of specific continents, countries, localities in modern world

These unassigned numbers may be used for the new subjects/concepts. However, such hospitality may not always provide appropriate places for the concepts and, therefore, can break the grouping order.

## Types of bibliographic classification scheme

At one extreme, a classification scheme can be completely enumerative: every subject and class is listed with a predefined notation and the classifier has simply to choose a class and the corresponding notation. At the other extreme, a classification scheme can be fully faceted: the classifier has to follow a set of rules to construct a class number. In between these two extremes there is a classification scheme that to some extent is enumerative yet at the same time makes provisions for some sort of synthesis to build the class number; these are called analytico-synthetic classification schemes. Library of Congress (LC) classification is a typical example of enumerative classification, Universal Decimal Classification (UDC) is a typical example of an analytico-synthetic classification scheme and Colon Classification (CC) is an example of a faceted classification scheme.

## Enumerative classification schemes

In an enumerative classification scheme, all the possible classes are enumerated. A top-down approach is implemented here: subordinate classes are produced. Both simple and complex subjects are listed. The advantage is that the structure of the scheme is shown by the notation as far as practicable. Users can easily find the superordinate, coordinate and subordinate classes and then make a mental map of the subject. The disadvantage is that it is difficult to accommodate new subjects, and regular revisions may be required. An enumerative classification scheme, in some cases, displays hierarchical notation structures. For example in DDC:

641.5 Cooking
641.52 Breakfasts
641.53 Luncheons, lunches, teas, suppers, snacks
641.54 Dinners
641.55 Money-saving and timesaving cooking
641.552 Money-saving cooking
641.555 Timesaving cooking

In the above example a hierarchy can be noted: 641.5→641.55→641.552. It may also be noted that 641.5 is the superordinate to 641.52, 641.53, 641.54 and 641.55. The coordinate classes are 641.52, 641.53, 641.54 and 641.55, and 641.552 is subordinate to the 641.55 class.

The basic tenet of an enumerative classification is that all the possible subjects and topics are listed, along with a predefined class number, and therefore the classifier does not have to create any class numbers. Early classification schemes like DDC and LC were enumerative classification schemes, although over the years DDC has introduced many synthetic features and thus has become more like an analytico-synthetic classification scheme, although LC has largely remained the same and is a typical example of an enumerative classification scheme.

While enumerative classification schemes make the life of a classifier easy by listing classes and corresponding notations, they have an inherent drawback in that they are very rigid, and the classifier is restricted to the classes that are listed. There is no provision for creating a class number. Another disadvantage of an enumerative classification scheme is that it contains repetitions – the same concept appears again and again in different subjects and classes, and therefore the classification schedule becomes very bulky.

## Analytico-synthetic classification schemes

Analytico-synthetic classification schemes resolve some of the problems of enumerative classification schemes. The idea behind an analytico-synthetic classification is that the subject of a given document will be divided into its constituent elements, and then the classification scheme will be used to find notations for each element – which will then be joined as per the prescribed rules to prepare the final class number. UDC is an example of an analytico-synthetic classification scheme: one can build numbers either by linking the numbers from the main classes or by adding numbers from the auxiliary tables. DDC also has some analytico-synthetic features: one can build class numbers by adding numbers from different tables or through the 'add notes'.

Analytico-synthetic classification schemes overcome the two major disadvantages of enumerative classification schemes: providing various tables, notational symbols and rules they avoid the need for a long list of classes, and thus the classification scheme in smaller; they also provide flexibility to users in that specific numbers can be built and the classifier is not restricted by the availability (or non-availability) of a specific subject.

Nevertheless, these schemes make classifiers' jobs complex because classifiers have to construct class numbers rather than just select them from a list.

## Faceted classification schemes

Instead of listing classes and their corresponding numbers, a faceted classification scheme lists the various facets of every subject or main class and provides a set of rules for constructing class numbers through facet analysis (an example is given in the following section).

| W | Political science |
|---|---|
| X | Economics |
| Y | Sociology |
| Z | Law |

The schedule of basic subjects also lists the subdivisions of these main subjects and a number of other subjects, such as:

| 01 | Generalia |
|---|---|
| 1 | Communication science |
| 2 | Library and information science |
| 3 | Book science |
| 4 | Mass communication |
| 5 | Exhibition technique |
| 6 | Museology/museum technique |
| 7 | Systems research |
| 8 | Management science |
| ... | |
| ... | |
| A | Natural sciences |
| AT | Laboratory service |
| ... | |
| AXB | Environmental sciences |
| ... | |
| ... | |
| B | Mathematics |
| B1 | Arithmetic |
| B2 | Algebra |

CC introduced the concepts of common and special isolates. Common isolates are those that can form part of any subject, and special isolates are those that form part of a specific subject. The common isolates in CC are: language isolates, time isolates, space isolates, common energy isolates, common matter-property isolates, common property isolates and anteriorizing common isolates (e.g. bibliographies, serials, encyclopaedias, case studies, etc.).

There are six phase relations in CC that can be used to denote relationships between the components of a complex subject. These phase relations are: general, bias, comparison, difference, tool and influencing. CC uses alphanumeric characters and punctuation marks as notational symbols. It also uses interpolation techniques to accommodate new isolates in an array; in other words, in order to accommodate a number of isolates within a range of notations, CC uses some special techniques for extending the capacity of the notations.

Examples of extrapolation in the main subjects are:

L     Medicine
LUD    Medical technology
LX    Pharmacognosy
M     Useful arts

Examples of extrapolation in the space isolates are:

44   India
44T  Nepal
44V  Ceylon
44X  Pakistan
45   Iran

CC uses a number of notational symbols as indicator digits to denote various isolates, facets and phase relationships, such as: ★ → ” & ‘ . : ; , - = +

In some cases, a combination of symbols is used to denote a specific isolate or relation; for example '&a' denotes intersubject general phase relation while '&b' denotes intersubject bias phase relation.

In order to build a class number in CC, one has first to analyse the various facets of the subject, and then their various rounds and levels have to be identified. Then the schedule has to be consulted to find the specific notations for each facet, and they are joined using appropriate indicator digits. The following example shows facet analysis and number building according to CC (Ranganathan and Gopinath, 1987).

Subject: Research into the cure of tuberculosis of the lungs by X-ray, conducted in India in the 1950s

Facet analysis: Medicine (BF). Lungs [1P]. Tuberculosis [1MP]. Treatment [1E]. X-ray [2MMt]. Research (CEI). India [S]. 1950s [T].

where Medicine is the basic subject (or basic facet, denoted as BF), 1P denotes the first round personality facet (here 'Lungs'), 1MP denotes the first round of the matter-property facet (here 'Tuberculosis), 1E denotes first round energy facet (here 'Treatment'), 2MMt denotes the second round matter-material facet (in this case 'X-ray'), CEI denotes common energy isolate (here 'Research'), S denotes space (here 'India') and T denotes time ('1950s'). The class number for this subject will be: L,45;421:6;253:f.44'N5.

The following are some examples of CC numbers for compound and complex subjects:

Difference between the psychology of men and women: S,51&w5

where '&w' denotes the intra-array phase relation between two components of the subjects men and women, in the psychology main subject, and

Influence of nourishment on education: T&gL;573

where '&g' denotes an intersubject influencing phase relation.

## Library of Congress Classification

The Library of Congress Classification (LC) was solely constructed for the Library of Congress from 1901 onwards (Chan, 1999). It provides a long list of all the classes in the universe of subjects. The following are some general features of LC. It:

- is enumerative in nature
- is based on literary warrant (LC was designed primarily to classify resources at the Library of Congress; in other words, it was built to classify subjects in the Library's collection)
- provides less flexibility for building class numbers by synthesis
- is also available on the web at http://classificationweb.net/
- is best suited for a large library like a university or a national library
- uses mixed notation
- has compound subjects pre-coordinated and listed
- has very limited scope of synthesis

- lacks hospitality
- has no provision for the construction of classes that are not listed
- suffers from repetition of concepts
- has very lengthy schedules
- includes the danger of cross–classification
- lacks mnemonic features
- has no explicit theoretical principles behind the organization of its basic classes
- is a broad classification used specifically for shelf arrangement
- is difficult to navigate but easy to apply.

The full text of LC is distributed by the Library of Congress's Cataloging Distribution Service in the following formats (Library of Congress, 2005):

- 41 printed volumes, called schedules, which may be purchased individually or as a set
- world wide web access via Classification WEB (http://classificationweb. net), an online product that includes not only LCC but also the text of Library of Congress Subject Headings (LCSH)
- a full set of LCC records in MARC 21 or MARCXML format, as well as subscriptions to a weekly update service.

LC divides the universe of knowledge into 21 basic classes, each identified by a single letter of the alphabet. Most of these basic classes are further divided into more specific subclasses, identified by a two–letter, or occasionally three–letter, combination. For example:

N   Art
NA   Architecture
NB   Sculpture
ND   Painting

The main classes of LC are as follows (Library of Congress, 2005):

A   General works
B   Philosophy. Psychology. Religion
C   Auxiliary sciences of history

D    History (general) and history of Europe
E    History: America
F    History: America
G    Geography. Anthropology. Recreation
H    Social sciences
J    Political science
K    Law
L    Education
M    Music and books on music
N    Fine arts
P    Language and literature
Q    Science
R    Medicine
S    Agriculture
T    Technology
U    Military science
V    Naval science
Z    Bibliography. Library science. Information resources (general)

The following are some examples of LC numbers:

Chemistry   QD
Selections from Shelley   PR5403
Selections from Wordsworth   PR5853
Labour   HD8039
Engineers   HD8039.E5
Love   BF575.L8
Hate   BF575.H3.

## Dewey Decimal Classification

In 1876 the first edition of Dewey Decimal Classification (DDC), entitled *A Classification and Subject Index for Cataloguing and Arranging the Books and Pamphlets of a Library*, was published. Melvil Dewey's name did not appear on the title page, but it was stated in the copyright notice on the verso of the title page; later it was officially known as Dewey Decimal Classification (Chan and Mitchell, 2003).

Over the years new editions of DDC have regularly appeared, each incorporating a number of improvements over previous editions. Currently DDC is available in its 22nd edition. It is in four volumes, the first of which provides an introduction to DDC followed by six tables; volumes 2 and 3 contain the schedules and volume 4 includes the relative index. The latter provides guidance on how to classify difficult areas and how to choose between related numbers. It is now available on the web, called *WebDewey*, which has replaced the earlier CD version *Dewey for Windows* (http://connexion.oclc.org).

DDC is the most widely used library classification system in the world. It is used in more than 200,000 libraries in 135 countries, and has been translated into over 30 languages; in the USA, 95% of all public and school libraries, 25% of all college and university libraries and 20% of special libraries use DDC (OCLC, 2006).

## General rules for classification in DDC

DDC proposes the following steps for classification (Chan and Mitchell, 2003; OCLC, n.d.):

1  Place a work where it will be the most useful to the user and to the permanent order.
2  Class a work by subject and then by form of presentation, except for literature. For example, a dictionary of library science will be classed with library science and not with dictionaries. Here the subject (library science) is more important than the form (dictionary).
3  Class a work of literature first by its language and then by form: 'English drama' will be classed first by English language literature, and then by form (poetry, drama, fiction, etc.).
4  Class a work in the discipline for which it is intended rather than the discipline from which the work derives.
5  Once a broad discipline is determined, follow the main schedule; the summaries may be of some help.
6  Do not use the number from the relative index right away; follow the hierarchy in the schedule.
7  Class a work dealing with interrelated subjects in the subject that is being acted upon (this is called the 'rule of application').
8  Class a work in the most specific number in the scheme.

**9** Class a work first by subject if there is a choice between subject and geographical region.

**10** Class a work that covers two subjects with the subject that has been given more emphasis or fuller treatment in the work. For example, if a book dealing with physics and chemistry emphasizes the latter, then class it with chemistry.

**11** If two subjects are equally emphasized in a work, class the work under the subject that appears first in the schedule (this is called the 'first of the two rule').

**12** If a work covers three or more subjects, class under a broader class that covers all the subjects treated in the work (this is called the 'rule of three').

**13** Avoid subdivisions beginning with 0 if there is a choice between 0 and 1–9 at the same point in the hierarchy of the notation; also avoid using 00 if there is a choice between 0 and 00.

**14** Use the interdisciplinary number provided in the schedules. While using such a number, make sure that the work contains significant material on the discipline in which the interdisciplinary number is present.

**15** If an interdisciplinary number is not given for an interdisciplinary subject, class it under the subject that has received the fullest treatment in the work.

**16** Use the table of last resort (in order of preference) as a guideline, if it is difficult to decide which order to use when different components or aspects of a topic are discussed in a document. In case of doubt use the following in order of preference: kind of things; parts of things; materials from which things, kinds or parts are made; properties of things, kinds, parts or materials; processes within things, kinds, parts or materials; operations upon things, kinds, parts or materials; and instrumentalities for performing such operations to build the numbers.

## Dewey main classes

In DDC, the universe of knowledge is divided into ten main divisions, each called a main class. Each class is divided again into ten divisions, and this goes on successively, leading to divisions and subdivisions of various disciplines, subjects and concepts: hence the term 'decimal classification'.

Schedules for classes 000–500 appear in volume 2, and the rest are in volume 3 of the printed version of DDC.

The main classes are as follows:

000  Computer science, information & general works
100  Philosophy and psychology
200  Religion
300  Social sciences
400  Language
500  Science
600  Technology
700  Arts and recreation
800  Literature
900  History and geography

## Dewey tables

The first volume of the DDC scheme includes six tables. Each contains a sequence of notations indicating various special concepts used repeatedly in a variety of subjects and disciplines. The notations in these six tables cannot be used independently, but can be used along with the main class numbers given in volumes 2 and 3. The tables cover the following:

T1   Standard subdivisions
T2   Geographic areas, historical persons and periods
T3   Subdivisions for the arts, individual literatures and specific literary forms
    T3A   Subdivisions for works by or about individual authors
    T3B   Subdivisions for works by or about more than one author
    T3C   Notation to be added where instructed in Table 3B, 700.4, 791.4 and 808–809
T4   Subdivisions for individual languages and language families
T5   Ethnic and national groups
T6   Languages

In order to build a Dewey class number:

**1**  Choose an appropriate main class number.

**2** Follow the instructions given in the schedule for choosing the appropriate class number, or for building a number by synthesis.

**3** If necessary, use Table 1 with a base number (a number from the schedule) to build specific numbers, even when there are no instructions (unless there are instructions to the contrary).

**4** Use Tables 2–6 only when there are specific instructions to use one or more of these tables in the schedules and/or tables.

A Dewey class number begins with a base number from the schedule. Class numbers can be built by synthesis only when instructions in the schedule make them possible (except for standard subdivisions from Table 1). There are four sources from which to build numbers by synthesis: by using Table 1 (standard subdivisions); by using Tables 2–6 (only when appropriate instructions are given); by taking numbers from other parts of the schedule (only when appropriate instructions are given); and by using the 'add table' instructions in the schedule (only when appropriate instructions are given).

The following examples show the use of tables along with the main class numbers.

### Table 1: standard subdivisions

This is a table of notations designating certain frequently recurring forms or methods of treatment applicable to any subject or discipline. Standard subdivisions are sometimes listed in the schedules when

- subdivisions have a special meaning
- extended notation is required for the topic in question
- notes are required.

Standard subdivisions are never used alone, but can be used any time at the end of the main class number from the schedule unless there is a specific instruction to the contrary. Note that more than one standard subdivision should not be used unless specifically instructed. There are specific rules regarding the use of zeros when using the tables along with the main class numbers. Some illustrations are given below, and the detailed rules and practices can be found in the introduction to Dewey and in the guidebook (Chan and Mitchell, 2003).

For example:

The HarperCollins concise encyclopedia of world religions  200.3

where 200 is 'Religion' and –03 is 'Encyclopedia' (from Table 1). Note that a 0 has been dropped, following the general rule that if a base number ends with a 0 then drop a 0 from the resulting number when a standard subdivision number is added.

Dictionary of human anatomy 611.003

where 611 is 'Human anatomy' and –03 is 'Dictionaries' (from Table 1). Note that an extra 0 has been added according to the instructions given under 611 in the schedule; this special instruction overrules the general rule for adding standard subdivision numbers, according to which the class number should have been 611.03.

## Table 2: geographical areas, historical periods and persons

Notations from this table can be used with notations from elsewhere in the schedules and tables. The notations can be used by using 'T1–09 Historical, geographic, persons treatment'.
For example:

Foreign policies of Ethiopia 327.63

where 327.3–.9 is 'Foreign relations of specific nations' and –63 is 'Ethiopia' (from Table 2). Note that the number has been constructed according to the instructions given under 327.3–.9 in the schedule.

Sheffield University library 027.742821

where 027.73–.79 is 'Libraries of specific institutions' and –42821 is 'Sheffield' (from Table 2). Note that the number has been constructed according to the instructions given under 027.73–.79 in the schedule.

## Table 3: subdivisions for the arts, individual literatures and specific literary forms

This table is used with notations from the literature class (class 800).

There are actually three tables: Table 3A, used for description, critical appraisal, biography, or single or collected works of an individual author; Table 3B, used for description, critical appraisal, biography, or the collected works of two or more authors; and also for rhetoric in specific literary forms; and Table 3C, used for notations to be added as instructed in Table 3B, 700.4, 791.4 and 808–809.

For example:

English drama 822

where 82 is 'English Literature' and 2 is 'Drama' (Table 3A).

History of German literature 830.9

where 83 is 'German literature' and –09 is 'History' (Table 3B).

A collection of English language literary works for children 820.809282

where 82 is 'English literature', 080 is 'Collections' (Table 3B; the instruction is given here to 'Add to T3B--080 notation T3C--001-T3C--99 from Table 3C') and 9282 is 'Children' (Table 3C).

## Table 4: subdivisions of specific languages or language families

This table is never used alone, but may be used as required when constructing numbers under subdivisions of specific languages or language families (class 400).

For example:

Pronunciation of Japanese words 495.6152

where 495.6 is '*Japanese language' (instructions are given to '* Add to base number as instructed under 420–490') and –152 is 'Spelling (orthography) and pronunciation' (Table 4).

Specialized English dictionary 423.1

where 42 is 'English language' (instruction says, 'Add to base number 42 notation T4--01-T4--8 from Table 4') and –31 is 'Specialized dictionary' (Table 4).

## Table 5: ethnic and national groups

This table can be used when instructed, or can be used by using the notation -089 from Table 1 with any number from the schedules.
   For example:

National psychology of Germans 155.8431

where 155.84 is 'National psychology of specific ethnic groups' (there is an instruction here to 'Add to base number 155.84 notation T5--05-T5--9 from Table 5') and –31 is 'Germans' (from Table 5). Note that this number has been constructed according to the instructions given under 155.84 in the schedule.

Ceramic arts of Chinese 738.089951

where 738 is 'Ceramic arts', -089 is 'Racial, ethnic, national groups' (from Table 1) and -951 is 'Chinese' (from Table 5). Note that this number has been constructed according to the instructions given under 738 in the schedule and under -089 in Table 1.

## Table 6: languages

The use of Table 6 is quite restricted; one applies it only when specifically instructed to do so in the schedules or in other tables.
   For example:

Translation of the Bible into the Spanish language 220.561

where 220.53–.59 is 'Translation of the Bible into other languages' and –61 is 'Spanish' (Table 6). Note that instructions are given under 220.53–.59 in the schedule to use notations -3–9 from Table 6.

Political conditions in French-speaking countries 320.917541 where 320.9 is 'Political conditions', -175 is 'Regions where specific languages predominate' (Table 2) and -41 is 'French' (Table 6). Note that the number has been constructed according to the instructions given under 320.9 in the schedule, and under -175 in Table 2.

## Special features of DDC

DDC has a number of special features, which are briefly discussed below (Chan and Mitchell, 2003; OCLC, n.d.).

### Dewey notation: hierarchy

Hierarchy is expressed through structure and notation. For example:

| | |
|---|---|
| 600 | Technology (applied sciences) |
| 630 | Agriculture and related technologies |
| 636 | Animal husbandry |
| 636.7 | Dogs |
| 636.8 | Cats |

### Dewey notation: synthetic features

For example:

Study and teaching of agriculture 630.7

The notation for study and teaching appears in Table 1 (-07 'Study and teaching') and is used to build this class number by synthesis.

### Dewey notation: mnemonic features

The following are some mnemonic examples, in this case, all end in 6:

Spanish language 460
History of Spain 946
Spanish philosophy 196
Newspapers in Spanish languages 076

## Dewey notes

A variety of notes are provided in DDC, for example for building numbers by synthesis, for using alternative numbers, etc. There are various types of notes: some examples are given below.

- scope notes, such as 300 Social sciences ('Class here behavioral sciences, social studies')
- definitions, such as 200 Religion ('Beliefs, attitudes, practices of individuals and groups with respect to the ultimate nature of existences and relationships within the context of revelation, deity, worship')
- example notes, such as 027.68 Libraries for non-profit organizations ('including libraries of learned societies, museum libraries, United Nations Library')
- class here notes, such as 027.4★ Public libraries ('Class here public library branches') and 551.84 Hydrology ('Class here hydrological cycle, limnology, water balance')
- class elsewhere notes, such as 027.4★ Public libraries ('Class public library units for special groups and organizations in 027.6') and 551.48 Hydrology ('Class water resources, interdisciplinary works on water in 553.7')
- inclusion notes, such as 025.45 Orientation and bibliographic instructions for users ('Including signs, regulations for use, user manuals') and 370.15 Education for social responsibility ('Including critical pedagogy, education for democracy, popular education (education for socioeconomic transformation); social education').

## Add instructions

Add instructions in DDC are special instructions that have to be followed to build numbers by synthesis. Add instructions appear in the form of notes under specific classes in the schedule. Sometimes instructions are marked by a special symbol, for example:

616.927 ★Salmonella infections
    ★*Add as instructed under 616.1–616.9.*
     583–588 Specific taxonomic groups of plants
      583 ★Magnoliopsida (Dicotyledons)

584 *Liliopsida (Monocotyledons)
*Except for modifications shown under specific entries, add to each subdivision identified by * as follows: ...*

## Centred headings

These are non-coordinate DDC classes in which the hierarchical structure cannot be closely observed. For instance, in the following example the hierarchy of the classes has not been expressed through the notations; see, for example, classes 562 and 563 and their further subdivisions.

| | | |
|---|---|---|
| 500 | Science | |
| 560 | | Fossils and prehistoric life |
| 562–569 | | Specific taxonomic groups of animals |
| 562 | | Fossil invertebrates |
| 563 | | Miscellaneous fossil marine and seashore invertebrates |
| 564 | | Fossil Mollusca and Molluscoidea |
| 565 | | Fossil Arthropoda |
| 566 | | Fossil Chordata |
| 567 | | Fossil cold-blooded vertebrates, fossil Pisces (fishes) |
| 568 | | Fossil Aves (birds) |
| 569 | | Fossil Mammalia |

## Cross references

Both types of cross reference – 'see' and 'see also' – are used in DDC. See references direct the classifier to the correct number to be used. For example:

For welfare institution libraries, see 027.66
For stereoscopic projection, see 778.4

See also references are used to instruct the classifier to look for closely related numbers which may be an alternative. For example:

See also 001.422 for analysis of statistical data
See also 001.4226 for methods of presenting statistical data

## Dots and spaces

The dot and the space are used in DDC numbers to aid reading of the numbers. A dot is used between the third and the fourth digits, and a space is used in the schedules and tables after every three digits (these spaces aid in reading the class numbers; however, such spaces are not shown in the examples provided in this chapter).

## Local emphasis

In some classes, instructions are given for constructing class numbers to suit the needs of local users. For example:

750            Painting
759               Historical, geographic, persons treatment
759.1–759.9                 Geographic treatment

To give local emphasis and a shorter number to a work about painting and the paintings of a specific country, use one of the following options:

- a letter or other symbol for the country, e.g., Burmese painting and paintings 759.B (preceding 759.1)
- class them in 759.1; specifically painting and paintings of North America (in 759.97).

## Dewey relative index

A relative index is an alphabetical list that relates subjects to disciplines. It helps to bring together or collocate the different aspects of any particular subject. The relative index includes most of the terms found in the schedules and tables. For example, searching for 'Information management' will give the following results:

Information management—executive management    658.4038
Information management—military administration    355.688
Information management—office services    651
Information management—production management   658.5036
Information management—public administration    352.38

## WebDewey

The WebDewey database includes the most current version of the Dewey Decimal Classification (DDC 22 and all updates since its publication in 2003), plus supplemental data. It is updated quarterly (see http://connexion.oclc.org). It mainly contains records for Dewey entry numbers from the schedules and tables, records for entries in the DDC manual, the DDC relative index and Library of Congress subject headings (LCSH) associated with Dewey class numbers.

WebDewey gives additional points of access by combining Dewey numbers and Library of Congress subject headings. The other interesting feature is that it gives access to many pre-built numbers, especially in the literature class, which are not available in the print version. The following are some important features of WebDewey (Chan and Mitchell, 2003; OCLC, n.d.), which:

- provides browse options through DDC numbers, the relative index (pre-coordinated), LCSH (pre-coordinated), LCSH (KeyWordInContext, or KWIC), relative index (KeyWordInContext) and LCSH (editorially mapped)
- displays the main classes and the tables
- displays the hierarchical relationships along with coordinate–superordinate–subordinate classes
- provides flexible browsing and searching via different functionalities like limiting by index (combined-term searches in one or multiple indexes)
- provides options to search through all fields, all Dewey, DDC numbers, captions, the relative index, LCSH, LCSH (editorially mapped) and notes
- provides access to related records and entries cited in notes through hyperlinks
- links between LCSH listed in a record and the corresponding subject authority records.

WebDewey is available through the OCLC Connexion service (http://connexion.oclc.org). There are three basic options: the user can search (Figure 5.1) or browse (Figure 5.2) for a subject or class number or can simply go to the Dewey schedule or tables, from the search or the browse screen, and follow the hierarchy of the classes. Figures 5.3 and 5.4

(overleaf) show the search results from the Dewey relative index (for the search term 'information management') and the Dewey schedule (on the class '025').

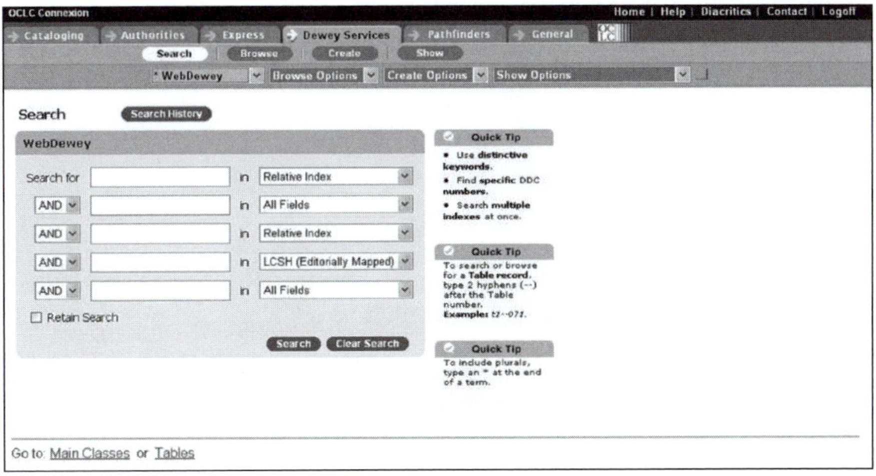

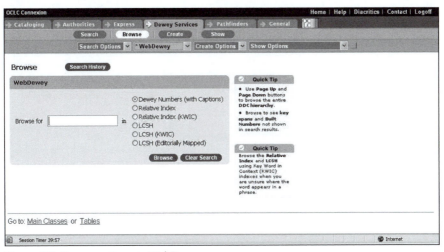

**Figure 5.1** Search options in WebDewey

**Figure 5.2** Browse options in WebDewey

**Figure 5.3** WebDewey search results (for 'information management') in the relative index

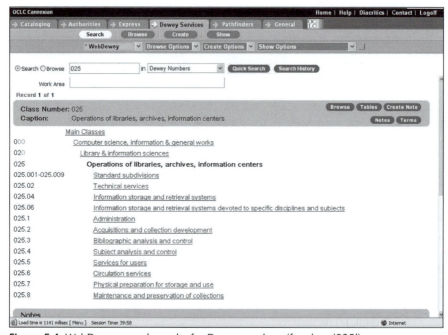

**Figure 5.4** WebDewey search results for Dewey numbers (for class '025')

## Universal Decimal Classification

In 1905, two Belgians, Paul Otlet and Henri La Fontaine, with the original intention of creating a universal bibliography of printed documents, developed the Universal Decimal Classification (UDC) scheme, based on the fifth edition of DDC (Foskett, 1996). UDC is now the second most widely used classification scheme in the world. The scheme contains over 56,000 main classes and over 13,000 common auxiliary classes (www.udcc.org/). The following are some general features of UDC (McIlwaine, 2000):

- It is basically an enumerative scheme, but it has many synthetic devices grafted onto its main core, which results in a great deal of flexibility. It is therefore analytico-synthetic in nature.
- The notation generally displays a hierarchy.
- UDC is in worldwide use, and has been published in whole or in part in 23 different languages.
- UDC uses mixed notations – numeric characters plus alphabets and punctuation marks.
- The arrangement is based on decimals.
- Every number is thought of as a decimal fraction with the initial point omitted.
- An advantage of this system is that it is infinitely extensible, and new subdivisions can be introduced without disturbing the existing allocation of numbers.
- The main classes mirror the main classes of DDC, apart from class 4 (which is left empty) and class 8 (language and literature grouped together).
- Simple subjects, and the relations between subjects, can be expressed.
- Special auxiliaries are important in the language and literature class and in many other classes.

Until 1992, UDC was managed by the FID (International Federation for Documentation), after which a consortium of UDC publishers (UDCC) was formed. Since 1992 the UDCC has been maintaining the scheme. A database called the UDC MRF (Master Reference File) is available from the UDC Consortium (UDCC, 2006). A two-volume edition of UDC was published by the British Standards Institution in 1993 (BSI 1000 M, 1993), followed by a pocket edition in 2003 (*UDC Abridged Edition*, 2003) and a full edition in 2005.

UDC contains main tables and auxiliary tables. The main table contains the main classes which are numbered 0–9:

0     Generalities
1     Philosophy. Psychology
2     Religion. Theology
3     Social sciences
4     Vacant
5     Natural sciences
6     Technology
7     The arts
8     Language. Linguistics. Literature
9     Geography. Biography. History

There are two types of auxiliary in UDC: common auxiliaries and special auxiliaries. Common auxiliaries are general in nature. They can be used in combination with the main tables or elsewhere if required, in any subject. The common auxiliaries are as follows:

Table 1c   Common auxiliaries of language
Table 1d   Common auxiliaries of form
Table 1e   Common auxiliaries of place
Table 1f   Common auxiliaries of ethnic grouping and nationality
Table 1g   Common auxiliaries of time
Table 1k   Common auxiliaries of properties; materials; relations, processes and operations; and persons and personal characteristics

Special auxiliaries express aspects that are recurrent, but over a limited subject range. They are therefore listed only in particular sections of the main tables. For example, the following special auxiliary table is enumerated in the arts class:

.01   Theory and philosophy of art
.02   Technique. Craftsmanship
.03   Artistic periods and phases. Schools, styles and influences
.04   Subjects for artistic representation. Iconography. Iconology
.05   Applications of art (in industry, trade, the home and everyday life)
.06   Various questions concerning art

.07 Occupations and activities associated with the arts and entertainment
.08 Characteristic features, forms, combinations etc. (in art, entertainment and sport)
.091 Performance, presentation (in original medium)

## Special signs in UDC

UDC uses a number of special signs as facet indicators.

A colon (:) is used to denote that there is some relationship between subjects, e.g.:

application of artificial intelligence in surgery 004.8:617

Note that the numbers should be joined in the order of their appearance in the schedule, but may be joined in any order as required. The sign is to be used to denote general or specific relations (like application, influence, comparison or difference) between two topics.

A plus sign (+) is used to link the notations representing two subjects, e.g.:

physics and chemistry: basic principles 53+54

Note that the sign is to be used when two subjects are treated in a document but their relationship is not specified.

A slash (/) is used to denote a range of consecutive classes, and is used between first and last numbers, e.g.:

A book of optics, heat and vibrations 534/536

Note that the plus sign can also be used to join the consecutive numbers, e.g.,

A book of optics, heat and vibrations 534+535+536

Square brackets ([]) are used to show a sub-grouping, and therefore to remove any ambiguity, e.g.:

Christianity in relation to Buddhism in India [23/28:294.3](540)

A double colon (::) is used for order-fixing, e.g.:

decorative handicrafts for interior decoration 747::745

where the double colon shows that no entry is required for decorative handicrafts. However, this is used rarely.

An equals sign (=) is used to denote language in which a document is written, e.g.:

Economic theory in French 330.1=133.1

Brackets containing a number beginning with zero (0...) are used to denote the form of the document, e.g.:

Conference proceedings in microbiology 579 (063)

A number placed within parenthesis is used to denote a place, e.g.:

Festivals in Canada 394.2(71)

An equals sign within parenthesis (=) is used to denote race, ethnic grouping and nationality, e.g.:

Social life of English-speaking people from cultural perspectives 316.7(=111)

Double quotation marks ("...") are used to denote the time, e.g.:

Agriculture in the 21st century 63"20"

A number preceded by -0 is used to denote general characteristics, e.g.:

Wooden floor 645.1-035.3

## Building UDC numbers

The following examples show how class numbers are built using some of UDC's synthetic devices:

Dictionary of physics 53(038)

Here, 53 stands for 'Physics' and (038) stands for 'Dictionary'. Note that the notation (0...) is used to denote a form division.

Electrical engineering and computer science 621.3 + 004

Note that + is used to link the notations representing two subjects.

Christianity in relation to Buddhism in India [23/28:294.3](540)

Here, 23/28 denotes the Christian religion (note that / is used to denote a range of subjects), : denotes a combination of notations implying relationships between subjects, 294.3 denotes 'Buddhism', square brackets are used for sub-grouping and (540) denotes 'India' (note that a place notation is always used in parenthesis).

A book on music written in Spanish 78=134.2

Here, 78 stands for 'Music' and 134.2 for 'Spanish' (in Table 1c). Note that = is used to denote language.

Periodicals on pharmacology 615(05)

Here, 615 is used for 'Pharmacology' and (05) for 'Periodicals' (from Table 1d).

Criminal law in Italy 343 (450)

Here, 343 stands for 'Criminal law' and (450) for 'Italy' (from Table 1e).

19th century architecture 72"18"

Here, 72 stands for 'Architecture' and "18" for '19th century' (from Table 1g).

## Bibliographic Classification

Bibliographic classification (BC) was originally devised by Henry Evelyn Bliss. It was first published in the 20th century (four volumes were published in the USA between 1940 and 1953; The Bliss Bibliographic Classification, 2004). The original classification was essentially enumerative in structure, though it had many synthetic features. In 1967 the Bliss Classification Association was formed in Britain and it was suggested that a new and completely revised edition of the full BC should be made available (The Bliss Bibliographic Classification, 2004). The new, revised edition (BC2) was initiated by Jack Mills and is to be produced in 22 parts, comprising one or two subjects per volume (Mills and Broughton, 1997–). Further revisions have been made to some of the BC2 volumes in order to retain subject currency, and the publication is now undertaken by Bowker-Saur. Updates appear in the *Bliss Classification Bulletin* (*BCA Bulletin*). BC2 is a fully faceted classification scheme. The major features of BC2 are as follows (The Bliss Bibliographic Classification, 2004):

- The main class order is based on theoretical principles.
- As CC is based on the five fundamental categories (personality, matter, energy, space and time) of Ranganathan (Ranganathan and Gopinath, 1987), BC2 is based on 13 categories in the following order: thing – kind – part – property – material – process – operation – patient – product – by-product – agent – space – time.
- Citation ordering is observed in such a way that the position of any compound class highly predictable.
- The filing order of general to specific is consistently maintained.
- BC2 is fully faceted and provides full synthetic features.
- The notational base consists of 35 characters: 1–9 and A–Z. BC2 does not use any other symbols or punctuation marks. For example, the class number for a work on 'Nurses as 'caregiver' for terminal patients and their families' is HPK PEY FBG K.
- Alphabetical indexes to all classes are provided, using Ranganathan's principles of chain indexing (Foskett, 1996; Ranganathan and Gopinath, 1987).
- BC2 provides a great deal of flexibility in classification, so that the needs of the local users can be met.

## Classification of electronic resources

Although classification schemes were mainly designed for organizing bibliographic items on library shelves, many researchers have also used library classification schemes to organize information resources on the web. Examples of such applications include CyberDewey (www.anthus.com/cyberdewey/cyberdewey.html) and CyberStacks (www.public.iastate.edu/). Some of these applications, though quite novel at the time of their development, are no longer updated.

Many live and heavily used digital libraries and subject gateways use bibliographic classification schemes to organize internet information resources, examples being BUBL (uses DDC) and the ACM digital library (uses ACM classification).

## BUBL (www.bubl.ac.uk)

BUBL uses DDC as the primary organizational structure for its catalogue of internet resources. Figure 5.5 shows the main catalogue of BUBL resources, organized according to the Dewey main classes; the user can click on any class to get to the corresponding subcategories, which are again arranged according to Dewey number.

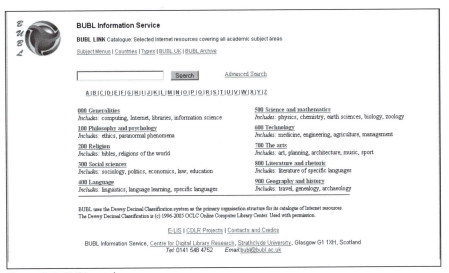

**Figure 5.5** BUBL catalogue

## CyberStacks

CyberStacks (www.public.iastate.edu/) is a centralized, integrated collection of selected digital resources categorized using the Library of Congress classification scheme. Using an abridged version of LC, Cyberstacks allows users to browse through virtual library stacks containing monographic or serial works, files and databases to identify potentially relevant information resources. Resources are categorized first within a broad classification, then narrower subclasses. Although Cyberstacks is the only site using LC and is a novel application in that respect, it has not been updated for some time.

## Specialized classification schemes

In addition to the traditional classification schemes, a number of special classification schemes have been devised to organize information resources in particular subjects/disciplines. The main reason behind this is that the traditional schemes are unable to provide sufficient detail in any specific area; so special classification schemes are becoming popular. They can deal with the specialized topics/vocabulary of a subject and can therefore meet user requirements. However, some drawbacks may restrict the use of special classification schemes, such as irregular revision, and limited documentation regarding support, training, etc. The ACM Classification scheme (www.acm.org/class/1998/ccs98.html) is one of these special classification schemes, and its main classes are listed below:

A General literature
B Hardware
C Computer systems organization
D Software
E Data
F Theory of computation
G Mathematics of computing
H Information systems
I Computing methodologies
J Computer applications
K Computing milieux

The ACM digital library uses the ACM classification scheme to help users access its information resources. After conducting a normal search using the search interface, when the user selects a specific retrieved item, they can see how the chosen search term appears in the ACM classification, and this may help them modify their query by selecting the appropriate category. Figure 5.6 shows a section of the ACM classification that appears when the user conducts a search on 'information retrieval' and selects a retrieved record; Figure 5.7 shows the same when the user chooses to search using another term, 'digital libraries'.

---

**Primary Classification:**
  **H.** Information Systems
      **H.3** INFORMATION STORAGE AND RETRIEVAL
        **H.3.3** Information Search and Retrieval
        **Subjects:** Retrieval models

**Additional Classification:**
  **I.** Computing Methodologies
      **I.2** ARTIFICIAL INTELLIGENCE
        **I.2.4** Knowledge Representation Formalisms and Methods
      **Subjects:** Semantic networks
      **I.5** PATTERN RECOGNITION
        **I.5.1** Models
        **Subjects:** Fuzzy set

---

**Figure 5.6** Section of ACM classification (on 'information retrieval')

---

**Primary Classification:**
  **H.** Information Systems
      **H.3** INFORMATION STORAGE AND RETRIEVAL
        **H.3.7** Digital Libraries

---

**Figure 5.7** Section of ACM classification (on 'digital libraries')

## Social classification or folksonomy

Given the complexities and resource-intensiveness of bibliographic classification systems, some alternative approaches to classifying electronic resources have evolved over recent years. This unstructured or freely structured approach to classification, with users assigning their own labels is variously referred to as 'folksonomy', 'folk classification', 'ethnoclassification', 'distributed classification', 'social classification', 'open tagging', 'free tagging' and 'faceted hierarchy' (Hammond et al., 2005). Folksonomy may be defined as a user-based approach to organizing information that consists of collaboratively generated, open-ended labels created by users to categorize web information resources.

Examples of folksonomy or ethnoclassification are del.icio.us (http:// del.icio.us/), which is a user-driven system for organizing online information resources, and flicker (www.flickr.com/), an online photo management and sharing application. A folksonomy allows users easily to add web pages of their choice to their personal collection of links, to categorize those sites with keywords and to share the collection with others. Thus, although folksonomies are often considered to be relatively non-standard and unsophisticated from the library and information science perspective, they are user-driven and make more sense to the user community, since the tags are assigned by users according to their understanding and use of concepts and documents.

## Summary

Modern library classification systems have a history going back over 125 years. Several general and special classification schemes have been developed over this period. Classification schemes differ from one another in a number of ways, but they all have the same objective – to enable a classifier to assign a class number to a document that represents the content of the document as closely as possible, and thus to assign a specific shelf location to the items.

Although classification schemes were mainly designed for organizing bibliographic items on library shelves, many researchers have also used library classification schemes to organize information resources on the web. Some of these applications were relatively small-scale research projects with small test collections, like CyberDewey and Cyberstacks, and have not been updated for quite some time. However, many live and heavily used information services and subject gateways also use bibliographic classification schemes to organize internet information resources, examples being BUBL and the ACM digital library.

Avoiding the resource-intensiveness and complex structures of bibliographic classification systems, some new unstructured (or freely structured) classification systems, called folksonomies, have appeared in the recent past that allow users to classify web resources using their own terms and categories. It will be interesting to see whether these so-called social classification systems can help people bring real order to the huge volume and variety of information resources on the web.

## REVIEW QUESTIONS

**1** What is a library classification scheme and what role does it play in organizing bibliographic information?

**2** In the context of library classification, what is a notation and what qualities should be possessed by a good system of notation?

**3** What are the main characteristics of an enumerative classification scheme?

**4** What are the main characteristics of a faceted classification scheme?

**5** What are the major differences between an enumerative and a faceted classification scheme?

## References

ACM Classification, www.acm.org/class/1998/ccs98.html.

The Bliss Bibliographic Classification (2004) www.sid.cam.ac.uk/bca/bcahome.htm.

BSI 1000 M (1993) *Universal Decimal Classification. International Medium Edition. English Text*, British Standards Institution.

BUBL Information Service, www.bubl.ac.uk.

Chan, L. M. (1999) *A Guide to the Library of Congress Classification*, 5th edn, Libraries Unlimited.

Chan, L. M. and Mitchell, J. (2003) *Dewey Decimal Classification: principles and application*, 3rd edn, OCLC.

CyberDewey, www.anthus.com/cyberdewey/cyberdewey.html.

CyberStacks, www.public.iastate.edu/.

Foskett, A. C. (1996) *The Subject Approach to Information*, 5th edn, Library Association Publishing.

Hammond, T., Hannay, T., Lund, B. and Scott, J. (2005) Social Bookmarking Tools (I): a general review, *D-Lib Magazine*, **11** (4), www.dlib.org/dlib/april05/hammond/04hammond.html.

Library of Congress (2005) *Cataloguing Policy and Support Office. Library of Congress Outline*, www.loc.gov/catdir/cpso/lcco/lcco.html.

McIlwaine, I. C. (2000) *The Universal Decimal Classification: a guide to its use*, UDC Consortium.

Mills, J. and Broughton, V. (1997–) *Bibliographic Classification*, 2nd edn, Butterworth/Bowker-Saur.

OCLC (2006) Dewey Services, www.oclc.org/dewey/.

OCLC (n.d.) *Introduction to Dewey Decimal Classification*, www.oclc.org/dewey/versions/ddc22print/intro.pdf.

Ranganathan, S. R. and Gopinath, M. A. (1987) *Colon Classification*, 7th edn, Sarda Ranganathan Endowment for Library Science.

Satija, M. P. (1989) *Colon Classification: a practical introduction*, 7th edn, Ess Ess Publications.

*UDC Abridged Edition* (2003) British Standards Institution.

UDC Consortium (2006) *Master Reference File*, www.udcc.org/mrf.htm.

Universal Decimal Classification (2005) *Complete Edition*, British Standards Institution.

# 6
# Subject heading lists and thesauri in information organization

## Introduction

Vocabulary control tools are used to control the terms used in indexing and information retrieval. These are natural language tools. Classification schemes, being tools for organizing information, could be of great help for vocabulary control – but the main body of a classification scheme uses a system of notation, an artificial language, whereas for vocabulary control we need natural language representation. Subject heading lists and thesauri are therefore used as vocabulary control tools for indexing printed and electronic information resources. This chapter begins with a discussion of the concept of vocabulary control tools, and outlines their typical features. It then considers the attributes of subject heading lists and describes the essential features of the most widely used one, the LCSH (Library of Congress Subject Heading list). It then goes on to outline the essential characteristics of thesauri and their role in information organization and retrieval, and illustrates this with examples from some online thesauri. The chapter then considers the role played by subject heading lists and thesauri in the organization and retrieval of electronic information, with examples from some special digital collections and subject gateways, especially the Intute subject gateways in different disciplines.

## Vocabulary control tools

According to Davis and Rush (1979), indexing may be thought of as a process of labelling items, and considerable order can be introduced into the process by standardizing the terms that are used as labels. This standardization – the systematic selection of appropriate terms – is known as vocabulary control.

Lancaster (2003) comments that a controlled vocabulary is basically an authority list with a specific structure that is designed to:

- control synonyms
- distinguish between homographs
- link terms based on their meaning.

We can define a vocabulary control tool as an organized list of terms and phrases that can be used to assign subject descriptors to information resources, and also (at least in some cases) to search a collection by subject terms and phrases. Subject headings lists like the Library of Congress Subject Headings (LCSH) and thesauri like the UNESCO thesaurus (ULCC, 2003a) are examples of vocabulary control tools.

## Subject heading lists and thesauri

A subject heading list is an alphabetical list of terms and phrases, with appropriate cross references and notes, that can be used as a source of headings in order to represent the subject content of an information resource. Although primarily arranged alphabetically, under each term or phrase we can find a list of other terms or phrases that are semantically related. LCSH is an example of a subject heading list; it is used quite widely as a controlled vocabulary for catalogues and bibliographies.

Subject heading lists were designed to complement bibliographic classification: while a bibliographic classification scheme helps us to assign a class number (built of notations) to an information resource that represents its subject content, a subject heading list allows us to assign an appropriate heading – as a term or a phrase – to an information resource that represents its subject content. A list of subject headings, or a subject index as it is often called, can be used to search or browse a collection of information resources. Subject heading lists help us produce a pre-coordinated index for a collection.

Subject indexing systems are broadly classified as pre-coordinate and post-coordinate systems. In both systems, the subject of a document is analysed and representative keywords are determined. In a post-coordinate system these keywords are not combined: the user may use any or all of them when searching. In contrast, in a pre-coordinate system, the keywords are syntactically combined, in a way that shows how the subjects relate to each other. Subject heading lists are examples of pre-coordinate systems: the subject terms are arranged in a predetermined order.

A thesaurus contains an organized set of terms, usually arranged alphabetically with appropriate cross references and notes. Thesauri have been developed for specific subject fields with a view to bringing together various representations of terms (synonyms, spelling variants, homonyms, etc.) along with an indication of a mapping of that term in the universe of knowledge by indicating the broader (superordinate), narrower (subordinate) and related (coordinate and collateral) terms.

Both subject heading lists and thesauri are examples of controlled vocabularies. They contain alphabetically arranged terms with necessary cross references and notes that can be used for indexing or searching in an information retrieval environment. However, there is a difference.

Subject heading lists were initially developed to be used in subject catalogues that could replicate the classified arrangement of library records, whereas thesauri have been developed in specific subject domains to facilitate indexing and retrieval. Lancaster (2003) comments that a subject heading list differs from a thesaurus because it has an imperfect hierarchical structure, and fails to distinguish between hierarchical and associative relationships.

## LCSH

LCSH stands for Library of Congress Subject Headings. LCSH was originally designed as a controlled vocabulary for representing the subject and form of the books and serials in the Library of Congress collection, with the objective of providing subject-based access to the bibliographic records in the library's catalogues.

LCSH is the most extensive list of subject headings. There are smaller lists: for example, the *Sears List of Subject Headings* (Miller and Goodsell, 2004) is a smaller work designed for small to medium-sized libraries.

LCSH contains the entry vocabulary of the Library of Congress catalogues. It is available in various formats including hard copy, CD-ROM and web. The latest edition is the 29th, which contains over 280,000 headings and references (Library of Congress, 2006). LCSH is the most widely used tool for assigning subject headings to manual and machine-readable catalogues. It is also now being used to control vocabulary in the virtual library environment; see, for example, INFOMINE, an academic virtual library located at the University of California, Riverside (INFOMINE, 1994).

The fundamental principles guiding the development of the LCSH are (Library of Congress, 1990):

1 User needs: Access points and current usage of terms are the two most important guiding factors. The objective of subject headings is to assist in the location of individual items in a collection. Subject headings should reflect the current usage of terminology in order to meet user needs.

2 Literary warrant (the literature on which the controlled vocabulary is based): LCSH headings are designed to index the collection of the Library of Congress. Hence, new subject headings, or links among existing headings, are created as they are needed to catalogue the materials being added to the collection.

3 Uniform headings: Each subject is represented by one heading, and this is followed consistently. Synonymous terms and variant forms of the same heading are considered non-preferred terms, and appropriate references are created to facilitate access to the collection by those terms.

4 Unique headings: Headings in LSCH are created such that each heading uniquely represents one subject; however, sometimes parenthetical qualifiers are used to distinguish homographs.

5 Specific and direct entry: According to LCSH the most specific term representing a subject is to be used as its heading; as a corollary, a subject is not entered under the broader or generic term that encompasses it.

6 Stability: Although it may sometimes be necessary to change some headings, this decision should be weighed against the impact and cost associated with such changes in terms of user inconvenience and in terms of re-cataloguing resources.

7 Consistency: Consistency in form and structure among similar headings is maintained, as far as practicable.

The approved subject headings in LCSH are set in bold face, while those in the entry vocabulary only, e.g. synonyms, appear in normal typeface. Each entry may be accompanied by all or some of the following:

- a scope note showing how the term may be used
- a list of headings to which 'see also' references may be made
- a list of headings from which 'see' references may be made
- a list of headings from which 'see also' references may be made.

Figure 6.1 shows an example of a typical entry in LCSH. A preferred term (appearing in bold face) is followed by an LC class number. There may also be a scope note, as appears under **Computer software**, which delineates the scope of the term/phrase.

---

**Computer software**
     [QA76.755]
 Here are entered general works on computer programs along with documentation such as manuals, diagrams and operating instructions, etc. ...
 UF     Software, Computer
 RT     Computer software industry
        Computers

       ...
 SA     *subdivisions* Software and Juvenile software *under subjects for actual software items*
 NT     Application software
        ....

        ....
        Systems software
         **- Accounting**
      [HF5681.C57]
            **-- Law and legislation**
               (May Subd Geog)
        **- Catalogs**
            UF Computer programs - Catalogs
        **- Development**
      [QA76.76D47]
       ...

**Figure 6.1** A typical LCSH entry

---

UF (used for) denotes the non-preferred headings for the given term/phrase, while BT, NT and RT denote broader, narrower and related terms, respectively. SA (see also) provides hints as to where related materials may be found. Some headings can be further subdivided geographically and this is indicated by the phrase 'May Subd Geog' immediately after the heading. A preferred heading may be subdivided to generate further appropriate preferred headings, e.g.: 'Computer software–Accounting' and 'Computer software–Accounting–Law and legislation'.

LCSH provides entries for USE/UF, NT/BT and RT/RT relations.

For example, the heading **Computer software** has 'Computer programs' as one of its NTs. So, if we look at the entry under **Computer programs** we find the heading 'Computer software' shown as the broader term (see Figure 6.2).

---

**Computer Programs**
    Here are entered works limited to computer programs …
    UF       Computer program files
               Files, Computer program
               …

               …
    BT       Computer files
               Computer software
               …

---

**Figure 6.2** LCSH reciprocal entries

Figure 6.3 shows an example of the output of a subject search from a typical OPAC. The subject search conducted was for 'digital libraries'; the results page shows the number of records available in the library under that specific heading in LCSH. This allows the user to get an idea of the various subheadings under the subject searched, and thus provides some sort of a map of the collection on this subject.

## Thesauri

Thesauri appeared in the late 1950s. They were designed for use with the emerging post-coordinate indexing systems of that time, which needed simple terms with low pre-coordination, not provided by the existing indexing languages (Aitchison, 1992). A thesaurus contains a controlled set of terms – from a particular area of knowledge – linked by hierarchical or associative relations; it also shows equivalence relations (synonyms) with natural language terms (Aitchison, Gilchrist and Bawden, 2000; Guinchat and Menou, 1983). Rowley (1994) defines a thesaurus as a compilation of words and phrases showing synonyms and hierarchical and other relationships and dependencies, the function of which is to provide a standardized vocabulary for information storage and retrieval systems.

From the two definitions given above we can see that a thesaurus is a tool containing a controlled set of terms arranged alphabetically, and

Search Request: Subject browse = digital libraries
Search Results: Displaying 1 through 40 of 40 entries.

◄ Previous   Next ►

| # | Hits | Heading | Heading Type |
|---|---|---|---|
| Display 1 | 26 | Digital libraries. | Library of Congress |
| Display 2 | 1 | Digital libraries Access control | Library of Congress |
| Display 3 | 3 | Digital libraries Administration | Library of Congress |
| Display 4 | 1 | Digital libraries Canada. | Library of Congress |
| Display 5 | 1 | Digital libraries Canada Case studies | Library of Congress |
| Display 6 | 1 | Digital libraries Collection and preservation. | General Heading |
| Display 7 | 2 | Digital libraries Collection development | Library of Congress |
| Display 8 | 7 | Digital libraries Congresses. | Library of Congress |
| Display 9 | 1 | Digital libraries Design | Library of Congress |
| Display 10 | 1 | Digital libraries Economic aspects. | Library of Congress |
| Display 11 | 1 | Digital libraries England Leicester. | Library of Congress |
| Display 12 | 1 | Digital libraries Europe Congresses | Library of Congress |
| Display 13 | 2 | Digital libraries Great Britain. | Library of Congress |
| Display 14 | 1 | Digital libraries Great Britain Case studies | Library of Congress |
| Display 15 | 6 | Digital libraries United States. | Library of Congress |
| Display 16 | 2 | Digital libraries United States Case studies | Library of Congress |
| Display 17 | 2 | Digital libraries United States Congresses. | Library of Congress |
| Display 18 | 18 | Digital mapping. | Library of Congress |
| Display 19 | 2 | Digital mapping Congresses | Library of Congress |
| more info Display 20 | 4 | Digital media. | Library of Congress |
| Display 21 | 1 | Digital media Access control Law and legislation Europe | Library of Congress |
| Display 22 | 1 | Digital media Access control Law and legislation Great Britain | Library of Congress |
| Display 23 | 1 | Digital media Great Britain | Library of Congress |
| Display 24 | 1 | Digital media Law and legislation Europe | Library of Congress |
| Display 25 | 2 | Digital media Law and legislation Great Britain | Library of Congress |

**Figure 6.3** Results of a subject search using LCSH in a library catalogue

various relationships among the terms are shown in order to facilitate indexing and retrieval. The major objective of a thesaurus is to exert terminology control when indexing, and to aid in searching by alerting the searcher to the index terms that have been applied.

According to Aitchison (1992), thesauri were recognized as widely used indexing tools with the first international standard for the construction of monolingual thesauri in 1974. Since then the processes of developing and maintaining thesauri have been standardized. There are international (ISO 2788:1986; ISO 5964:1985), British (BS 5723:1987; BS 6723:1985) and UNISIST standards (*UNISIST Guidelines*, 1980, 1981). BS 5723 has now been withdrawn and replaced by a new standard, BS 8723, of which two parts have been published thus far: BS 8723-1 (2005) and BS 8723-2 (2005). BS 8723 will have five parts, as follows, and when part 4 of BS 8723 comes out it will replace BS 6723:

BS 8723: Structured vocabularies for information retrieval
    Part 1: Definitions, symbols and abbreviations
    Part 2: Thesauri

Part 3: Vocabularies other than thesauri

Part 4: Interoperation between multiple vocabularies

Part 5: Interoperation between vocabularies and other components of information storage and retrieval systems.

Parts 1 and 2 of BS 8723 broadly correspond to ISO 2788 (1986). The fundamental aim of a thesaurus, according to BS 8723, is to guide indexers and searchers to choose the same term for the same concept. There are three major features of a thesaurus: vocabulary control, thesaural relationships and thesaurus display.

In a thesaurus all the concepts (words and phrases) in a given domain are listed. Some of these terms are valid index terms, called preferred terms: they can be used for the purpose of indexing. Others are called non-preferred terms: they cannot be used as valid index terms, and appropriate references are created from non-preferred to preferred terms to guide the indexer and the searcher. Thus preferred terms are used for indexing and searching, whereas non-preferred terms function as lead-ins to the preferred terms.

Thesauri have long been used for indexing online databases and almost all major online databases come with online thesaurus interfaces (Shiri, Chowdhury and Revie, 2002a, 2002b).

## Relationships between terms in a thesaurus

According to Aitchison (1992), there are two types of relationship in a thesaurus: first, macro-level relationships, which determine the arrangement of the whole domain of the thesaurus with its subject fields and subfields containing sets of hierarchically and associatively related terms; and, second, the inter-term relationships. Three general classes of fundamental thesaural relationships have been established:

■ the equivalence relationship
■ the hierarchical relationship
■ the associative relationship.

### Equivalence relationships

The equivalence relationship is to be found between preferred and non-preferred terms in an indexing language. It is denoted by USE (the prefix used for preferred terms) and UF (used for, the prefix used for non-preferred terms). This general relationship covers both synonyms and quasi-synonyms. Synonyms are terms whose meaning can be regarded as the same in a wide range of contexts, so that they are virtually interchangeable. There could be several cases of synonymity:

- terms with different linguistic origin, such as polyglot/multilingual
- popular names and scientific names, such as allergy/hypersensitivity
- variant spellings, such as encyclopaedia/encyclopedia
- terms from different cultures, such as flats/apartments
- abbreviations and full names, such as PVC/polyvinyl chloride
- the factored and unfactored forms of a compound term, such as coal mining/coal & mining.

Quasi-synonyms are terms whose meanings are generally regarded as different in ordinary usage, but which are treated as synonyms for indexing purposes, such as hardness and softness.

## Hierarchical relationships

The hierarchical relationship is the basic relationship that distinguishes a systematic thesaurus from other organized lists of terms (such as subject heading lists). Pairs of terms are represented in their superordinate or subordinate status, the superordinate term representing the whole and the subordinate term representing a member or a part. It may also represent thing–kind or genus–species or item–instance relations. The superordinate term is represented by BT (broader term), and the subordinate term by NT (narrower term). In a thesaurus a superordinate/subordinate pair is represented reciprocally as follows:

CAPITAL MARKETS
BT Financial markets

FINANCIAL MARKETS
NT Capital markets

There are three relational situations representing hierarchical relationships:

- the generic relationship
- the hierarchical whole–part relationship
- the polyhierarchical relationship.

The generic relationship identifies the relationship between a class or category and its member species. This relationship has a 'hierarchical force' – whatever is true of a given class is also true of all classes subsumed under it.

The hierarchical whole–part relationship covers a limited number of classes of terms in which the name of the part implies the name of the whole regardless of context (i.e. one concept is inherently included in another), so that the terms can be organized as logical hierarchies.

The polyhierarchical relationship occurs when a concept belongs to more than one category. For example:

PRINTING EQUIPMENT   COMPUTER PERIPHERAL
EQUIPMENT
    NT Computer printers
    NT Computer printers

COMPUTER PRINTERS
    BT Computer peripheral equipment
    BT Printing equipment

## Associative relationships

An associative relationship is neither hierarchical nor equivalent, yet the terms involved are associated to such an extent that the link between them should be made explicit in the thesaurus. This can reveal alternative terms, or coordinate terms, that could be used for indexing or retrieval. This relationship is reciprocal and is represented by RT. This relationship is the most difficult to define and therefore to determine. BS 8723-2 (2005) provides a general guideline that one of the terms should always be implied, according to the common frames of reference shared by the users of an index, whenever the other is used as an indexing term.

## Display of terms in a thesaurus

Terms and their relationships in a thesaurus can be displayed in one of the following ways:

- alphabetical display, with scope notes and relationships indicated for each term
- systematic display with an alphabetical index
- graphic display with an alphabetical index.

In an alphabetical display all indexing terms, whether preferred or non-preferred, are organized in a single alphabetical sequence. BS 8723-1 (2005) proposes a number of symbols and abbreviations for use in a thesaurus, such as:

- SN: scope note
- DEF: definition
- HN: history note
- USE: indicates that the following term is the preferred term
- UF: use for – indicating that the following term is the non-preferred term
- USE+: indicates that the two or more preferred terms following should be used together to represent the indicated concept
- UF+: indicates that the non-preferred term that follows should be represented by a combination of preferred terms including the preferred term that precedes UF+
- TT: top term
- BT: broader term
- BTG: broader term (generic)
- BTI: broader term (instantial, i.e. showing an instance, e.g.: capital cities and London)
- BTP: broader term (partitive, i.e. showing a whole–part relationship, e.g.: nervous system and central nervous system)
- NT: narrower term
- NTG: narrow term (generic)
- NTI: narrower term (instantial)
- NTP: narrower term (partitive)
- RT: related term.

The alphabetical form of a thesaurus is easy to organize. However, this form has a shortcoming from the user's point of view, as all the broader and narrower terms that constitute a hierarchy cannot be surveyed at once in an alphabetical thesaurus. Extra relational information can be added to an alphabetical display, such as the top term in the hierarchy to which a specific concept belongs. Similarly, the level of subordination and superordination can also be shown using BT1, BT2, NT1, NT2, etc.

Figure 6.4 shows a typical example of an entry in a thesaurus (ULCC, 2003b). It includes a preferred term (**Information/library planning**), a reference from a non–preferred term (Library planning), and the narrower terms Information/library economics and Information/library budgets at two different levels, designated by NT1 and NT2.

---

**Information/library planning**
Used For
       UF Library planning
Narrower Term
       NT1 Information and development
       NT1 Information/library cooperation
       *UF Information/library coordination, International library cooperation*
       NT1 Information/library economics
       *UF Library economics*
         NT2 Information/library budgets
         *UF Library budgets*
         NT2 Information/library finance
         *UF Library financing*
       NT1 Information/library resources
       NT1 Information/library statistics
       *UF Library statistics*

**Figure 6.4** A typical entry from the UNESCO thesaurus (ULCC, 2003b)

## Subject heading lists and thesauri in the organization of internet resources

While subject heading lists were primarily devised to assign subject headings in catalogues, many researchers have used them for organizing internet resources. Examples of some such efforts are given below.

## INFOMINE

INFOMINE is a service that provides access to several thousand web resources including databases, electronic journals, guides to the internet for most disciplines, textbooks and conference proceedings. It began in January 1994 as a project of the Library of the University of California at Riverside (Mitchell and Mooney, 1996). INFOMINE uses LCSH to index information resources. Users can simply select a discipline and enter their search terms or phrases to conduct a search. The catalogue can also be browsed by author, title, keyword and subject. There is an option to browse by subject – if this is chosen, the user is taken to an alphabetical list of subjects created by LCSH.

## Scout Report

The Internet Scout project is based at the University of Wisconsin-Madison and is part of the NSDL (National Science Foundation's National Science Digital Library) project. The project is funded by several bodies including the US National Science Foundation, the Andrew W. Mellon Foundation, Microsoft and the University of Wisconsin-Madison. 'Since 1994, the Internet Scout Project has focused on research and development projects that provide better tools and services for finding, filtering and delivering online information and metadata' (Internet Scout Project, 2006). The Scout Report Archive is a database containing 23,000 catalogued Scout Report summaries. It can be searched as well as browsed using LCSH (The Scout Archives, 2006).

## Intute: Health & Life Sciences

Intute: Heath & Life Sciences (2006), formerly BIOME, offers free access to a searchable catalogue of internet sites and resources covering the health and life sciences. Over 31,000 resource descriptions are listed, and freely accessible for keyword searching or browsing. Users can browse several subject collections such as: medicine, nursing and allied health, veterinary science, bioresearch, natural history, agriculture, food and forestry, etc. These collections can be browsed using one or more vocabulary control tools such as DDC, the CAB thesaurus, MeSH (Medical Subject headings) and the RCN (Royal College of Nursing) thesaurus.

Figure 6.5 shows the browse screen of Intute: Health & Life Sciences, where the user can choose to search a specific collection using a specific vocabulary control tool. After selecting a specific collection and the corresponding vocabulary control tool, the user sees an alphabetical list of subject headings along with the number of associated records in the collection (see Figure 6.6).

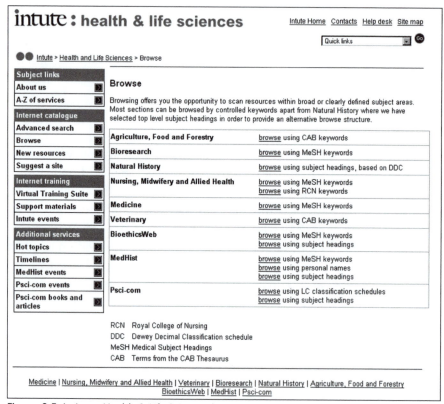

**Figure 6.5** Intitute: Health & Life Sciences browse screen

## Intute: Social Sciences

Intute: Social Sciences (2006), formerly SOSIG, is a subject gateway that provides free access to information resources in a large number of social science subjects including anthropology, economics, government, politics, geography, law, sociology, sports, statistics, etc. The collections can be browsed or searched using a number of vocabulary control tools: a general social science thesaurus (HASSET), a government, politics and anthropology thesaurus (IBSS), a social work and welfare thesaurus

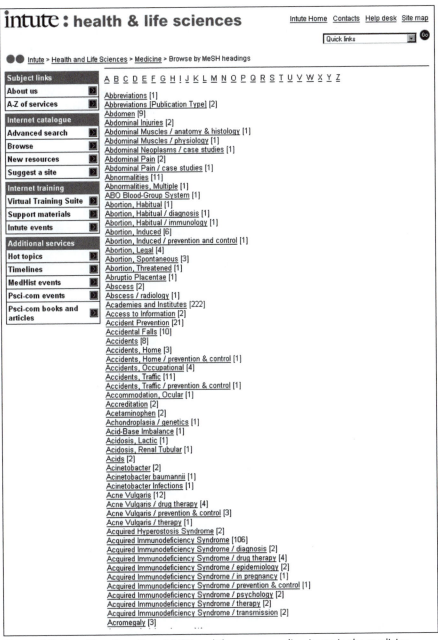

**Figure 6.6** List of headings from MeSH and the corresponding items in the medicine collection

(SCIE), a research methods and tools thesaurus (SRM) and the CAB thesaurus (CABI). Figure 6.7 shows the first screen of the Intute: Social Sciences site, where the user can select a specific subjct from a list. Users can choose to browse a subject and follow the links to access the records. Figure 6.8 shows the various subcategories of the subject of economics, the number of items corresponding to each subcategory and also some search results.

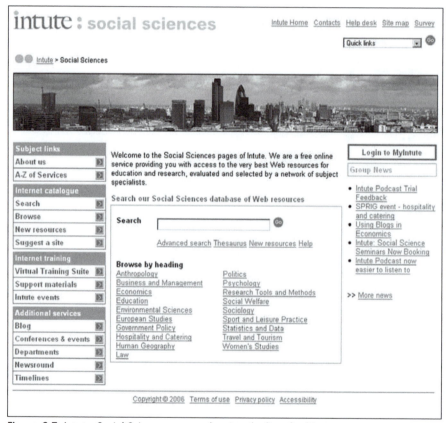

**Figure 6.7** Intute: Social Sciences screen showing the list of subjects

## Summary

Vocabulary control tools – subject heading lists and thesauri – are controlled natural language tools used to facilitate access to information by using pre-defined and pre-coordinated natural language terms. They play a key role in information organization and resource sharing, as they

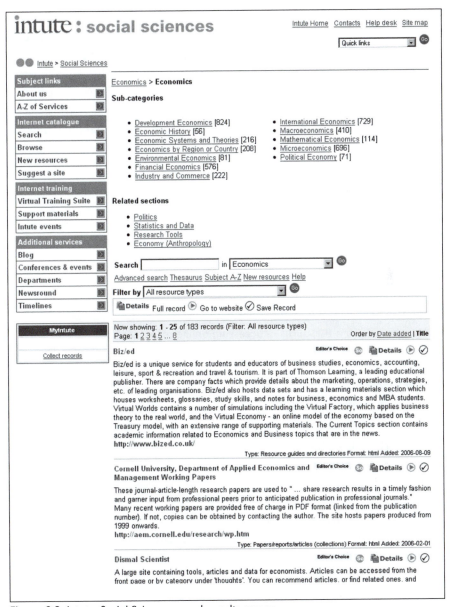

**Figure 6.8** Intute: Social Sciences search results screen

allow indexing agencies to use standard index terms. These tools also allow users to choose appropriate search terms when conducting and/or modifying a search. Although subject heading lists like LCSH are primarily used for indexing catalogue records, some researchers have also used them to index internet resources. Thesauri also play a key role in the indexing and retrieval of information in various disciplines contained in digital libraries and subject gateways like the Intute subject gateways.

There is another type of controlled vocabulary, in addition to thesauri and subject heading lists – ontologies. Ontologies are more sophisticated tools than thesauri and subject heading lists, and are can be used to organize information in web-based environments (see Chapter 12).

## REVIEW QUESTIONS

**1** What is a vocabulary control tool?
**2** What is a subject heading list and what role does it play in the organization of information?
**3** What is a thesaurus and what role does it play in the organization of information?
**4** What are the different relationships between terms in a thesaurus?
**5** How do we use a thesaurus in accessing online resources?

## References

Aitchison, J. (1992) Indexing Languages and Indexing. In Dossett, P. (ed.), *Handbook of Special Librarianship and Information Work*, 6th edn, Aslib.

Aitchison, J., Gilchrist, A. and Bawden, D. (2000) *Thesaurus Construction and Use: a practical manual*, 4th edn, Aslib.

BS 6723:1985 *Guidelines for the Establishment and Development of Multilingual Thesauri*, British Standards Institution.

BS 8723-1:2005 *Structured Vocabularies for Information Retrieval – Guide. Part 1: definitions, symbols and abbreviations*, British Standards Institution.

BS 8723-2:2005 *Vocabularies for Information Retrieval – Guide. Part 2: thesauri*, British Standards Institution.

Davis, C. H. and Rush, C. L. (1979) *Guide to Information Science*, Greenwood.

Guinchat, C. and Menou, M. (1983) *General Introduction to the Techniques of Information and Documentation Work*, UNESCO.

INFOMINE (1994) *Scholarly Internet Resource Collection*, http://lib-www.ucr.edu/.

Internet Scout Project (2006) http://scout.wisc.edu/.

Intute: Health & Life Science (2006) www.intute.ac.uk/healthandlifesciences/.

Intute: Social Sciences (2006) www.intute.ac.uk/socialsciences/.

ISO 2788:1986 *Guidelines for the Establishment and Development of Monolingual Thesauri*, International Organization for Standardization.

ISO 5964:1985 *Guidelines for the Establishment and Development of Multilingual Thesauri*, International Organization for Standardization.

Lancaster, F. W. (2003) *Indexing and Abstracting in Theory and Practice*, 3rd edn, Facet Publishing.

Library of Congress (1990) *Library of Congress Subject Headings – Principles of Structure and Policies for Application: contents*, www.itsmarc.com/crs/shed0014.htm.

Library of Congress (2006) *Library of Congress Subject Headings*, 29th edn, www.loc.gov/cds/lcsh.html.

Miller, J. and Goodsell, J. (2004) *Sears List of Subject Headings*, 18th edn, H. W. Wilson.

Mitchell, S. and Mooney, M. (1996) INFOMINE: a model web-based academic virtual library, *Information Technology and Libraries*, **15** (1), 20–5.

Rowley, J. E. (1994) The Controlled Versus Natural Indexing Languages Debate Revisited: a perspective on information retrieval practice and research, *Journal of Information Science*, **20** (2), 108–19.

The Scout Archives (2006) http://scout.wisc.edu/archives/index.php.

Shiri, A. A., Chowdhury, G. and Revie, C. (2002a) Thesaurus-enhanced Search Interfaces, *Journal of Information Science*, **28** (2), 111–22 .

Shiri, A. A., Revie, C. and Chowdhury, G. (2002b) Thesaurus-assisted Search Term Selection and Query Expansion: a review of user-centred studies, *Knowledge Organization*, **29** (1), 1–19.

ULCC (2003a) *UNESCO Thesaurus*, University of London Computer Center, www.ulcc.ac.uk/unesco/.

ULCC (2003b) *UNESCO Thesaurus: hierarchical list*, University of London Computer Center, www.ulcc.acuk/unesco//MTterms/515.htm.

*UNISIST Guidelines for the Establishment and Development of Multilingual Thesauri* (1980), rev. edn, UNESCO.

*UNISIST Guidelines for the Establishment and Development of Multilingual thesauri* (1981), 2nd edn, UNESCO.

# 7
# Organization of internet information resources

## Introduction

As discussed in previous chapters, over the years libraries have developed and used a number of organizational tools and techniques. These tools – classification schemes, catalogue codes, bibliographic formats and vocabulary control tools, and the corresponding standards for exchange formats like ISO 2709 – enable libraries to organize, provide access to and share millions of information resources throughout the world. Although these tools and standards were built to deal primarily with printed or physical records, some researchers have also tried to use them to organize internet information resources. Such applications have limited scope: although the traditional bibliographic tools and standards have huge merits, they are not quite suitable, at least in their usual form, for organizing internet information resources. But why so, and how can we organize internet information resources so that they can be easily accessed? This chapter aims to provide answers to some of these questions. It first explains why conventional bibliographic tools are not suitable for organizing internet resources. It then discusses a number of tools and techniques developed over the past few years for organizing internet resources.

## Characteristics of the web

Simply speaking, the web is a massive collection of pages or information resources stored on millions of computers across the world, which are linked by the internet. The uniqueness of web information organization and access has been widely discussed in the literature (e.g. Chowdhury, 2004; Rasmussen, 2002). The following are some unique characteristics of the web that call for special measures for the organization of the web information resources.

### Distributed nature of the web

Web information resources are distributed all over the world. Hence, complex measures are required to locate and organize these. A number of tools and standards – such as classification schemes, catalogue codes, MARC formats, subject heading lists, etc. – exist for organizing and providing access to networked library resources. Such uniform tools and standards are required for the organization and processing of web information resources.

### Size and growth of the web

The web has grown exponentially over the past decade. Identifying, organizing and retrieving information becomes more complex as the size of the web increases.

The resource intensiveness – too much dependence on human experts – of conventional information organization tools makes them unsuitable for handling the large volume of information on the web.

Information resources on the web can be accessed at two different levels. While millions of web information resources can be accessed by anyone, a significant volume of information is accessible only by authorized users (information that is password-protected, say). Researchers call the former the 'surface web' and the latter the 'deep web', and note that the deep web is several times larger than the surface web.

### Type and format of documents

Information files on the web can range from simple text to digital video, and each type can appear in a variety of formats, thereby making the task of organizing these information resources more complex and challenging.

### Control of information resources

Since anyone can publish almost anything on the web, it is very difficult to develop a centralized approach to organizing information resources, as is common in the bibliographic information world – where cataloguing and classification activities are performed centrally and resources are then shared among various libraries.

## Frequency of changes

Web pages change quite frequently, in terms of location, ownership, structure, contents, etc. This is in sharp contrast to traditional libraries that deal with relatively static information; once an information resource is added to a library's collection, the ownership, content, etc. do not change. Keeping track of web page changes, and making the necessary changes in the records, is not only a major challenge but is quite resource intensive too. A major problem with the web is that the resources (the web pages) often move. They need to be tracked regularly in order to keep the information relating to location up to date.

## Distributed users

The main principles of bibliographic information organization tools – such as catalogue codes, subject heading lists, classification schemes, etc. – have always been guided by user requirements. However, anyone, located anywhere in the world, can use an information resource on the web. This imposes a significant challenge, since it is difficult to organize resources for a heterogeneous group of users whose characteristics and needs can vary widely.

## Resource requirements

The organization of bibliographic information resources involving such tasks as recording, cataloguing, classifying and subject indexing has always been a human-dependent and resource-intensive process, both in terms of time and money. Centralized processing of information and resource sharing are practised in the library world in order to overcome this problem. Great amounts of resources would be required to organize properly the information resources on the web, if approaches similar to those prevailing in the library world were to be adopted. The situation is worsened by the fact that there is no single body that would fund these activities – and yet many want an organized collection for easy access to web information resources.

## Metadata: why not bibliographic formats?

In the library world, bibliographic formats, like MARC 21, are used to create a record for each item, and these records are used to exchange data and to create catalogue records. Bibliographic formats like MARC 21 prescribe a number of fields, subfields, etc., for each record. This makes the job of record creation very time-consuming and resource-intensive. Using such tools to organize millions of web resources would be an impossible task. Moreover, bibliographic formats do not prescribe fields, subfields, etc. that can be used to store information unique to web resources, such as multiple dates of creation or revision, provenance, terms of access and use, etc.

In order to overcome these problems, metadata standards have been developed. The primary function of a metadata standard is to facilitate the identification, location, retrieval, manipulation and use of digital objects in a networked environment (Gorman and Dorner, 2004; Haynes, 2004). In the mid-1990s the DCMI (Dublin Core Metadata Initiative) (DCMI, 2006) was established with a view to prescribing a core set of data elements required for creating catalogues of web resources. The DCMI defined a core set of 15 data elements that can be used as containers for metadata. It should be noted that the concept of a metadata system was not entirely originated by librarians, and 'librarians have had to share the metadata stage with other communities, each with its own concerns and own techniques of inform-ation management' (Campbell, 2004, 186). Details of the Dublin Core and other metadata standards and their applications appear in Chapter 8.

## Bibliographic classification schemes: are they suitable for organizing the web?

Although bibliographic classification schemes like DDC, UDC, LC, etc. have been used successfully for decades to organize millions of information resources in libraries, and also for organizing smaller and selected collections of internet resources, they have some inherent shortcomings that make them unsuitable for organizing the huge volume and variety of web information resources:

■ Bibliographic classification is fairly resource-intensive.
■ Its aim is to specify a shelf location for every information resource. It can specify only one location even if the item deals with more than one subject, which is a problem with resources on inter-disciplinary subjects.

- By assigning a specific notation or class number to a given document, bibliographic classification schemes can lead to too much abstraction. A classifier comes up with a brief subject description that is then represented by a class number; this is not altogether suitable for new and multidisciplinary subjects.
- Classification requires too much human intervention. A human indexer or classifier has to study the content of the item, come up with a brief description of the subject/topic, and then consult the classification scheme in order to assign a class number that represents (or closely represents) the content.
- The level of subject representation achieved depends on the classification scheme used. Bibliographic classification schemes are neither always up to date nor always specific enough for new and specific subjects and topics. Moreover, achieving international standards and procedures in amending existing classification schemes is a complex and often cumbersome process, thereby making it extremely difficult to keep classification schemes up to date.

Thus, it is not feasible to classify web information resources in the same way as bibliographic information resources – that is, by using human indexers. Automatic classification systems using clustering techniques have been used by some web search tools for organizing web resources – see for example Kartoo (www.kartoo.com) and Vivisimo (www.vivisimo.com) – but they are not as robust as the big search engines like Google.

## Subject heading lists: can they be used for indexing internet resources?

Subject heading lists, used to index bibliographic resources, contain pre-coordinated subject headings, but selecting an appropriate heading for the subject of a given information resource is not always an easy task. It is a resource-intensive process, in terms of both human involvement and time. As discussed in Chapter 6, some attempts have been made to index relatively small collections of web information resources using subject heading lists. However, subject heading lists suffer from two major problems: not being always up to date, and shortage of new, specific headings suitable for indexing the wide variety of web information resources. Thesauri also suffer from similar shortcomings; although some specific thesauri have been developed and are used for organizing web resources (see the Intute examples in Chapter 6), keeping thesauri up to date to meet the demands of the web environment is an uphill task. New tools comprising detailed, organized lists of both general and specific subject terms, and mechanisms for automatic assignment and updating of headings, will be more appropriate for organizing web information resources.

## New tools and standards for managing internet information

Web technologies have brought a revolution in the creation, distribution and use of information – not only scholarly information traditionally published in print, but also information of interest to all kinds of businesses and organizations. Every organization, not just academic and research institutions, now creates, stores, distributes and uses a variety of information resources through the internet or an intranet. These information resources vary in terms of file type and format, structure, content and terms of accessibility. The volume of such information is increasing at a rapid pace. No organization can improve its performance, or even can survive, in today's digital world without appropriate mechanisms for providing proper access to such resources. New systems, called content management systems, have been developed over the past few years to manage such information. Several tools and techniques, like information architecture, ontology and markup languages like XML and RDF, are used for content management activities. These new tools and technologies are discussed later in this book (Chapters 9–11).

## The semantic web

Although the vast amount of information on the web can now be browsed and searched using a number of sophisticated web search tools – directories and search engines – web information resources are still not semantically linked in a way that can facilitate semantic retrieval. Tim Berners-Lee's vision of the semantic web is of a web of information sources whose semantic contents or meanings are machine-readable (Berners-Lee, 2003). At the foundation of the semantic web there are several standards and technologies, including the resource description framework (RDF), uniform resource indicators (URIs), the OWL language and XML. The basic concept of the semantic web and the corresponding tools and technologies are discussed in Chapter 12.

## Summary

Bibliographic classification schemes, catalogue codes, bibliographic formats, vocabulary control tools and authority control files, and the corresponding standards, have long been used in libraries to organize, provide access to and share information resources. However, these techniques are very resource-intensive, and the tools are often not up to date or robust enough to meet the challenges of organizing the huge volume of information resources available on the internet. A number of tools and techniques have been developed in recent years to manage internet information sources. A major web development – the semantic web – is envisaged, which will enable all web-based information sources to be linked appropriately on the basis of their meaning (see Chapter 12).

## REVIEW QUESTIONS

1 What are the typical characteristics of the web that make the management of web information resources difficult?
2 Why are library classification schemes in their current form not suitable for organizing web information resources?
3 Why are catalogue codes in their present form not suitable for organizing web information resources?
4 Why are bibliographic formats in their present form not suitable for tagging web information resources?
5 What are the major difficulties of using general vocabulary control tools in organizing web information resources?

## References

Berners-Lee, T. (2003) Foreword. In Fensel, D., Hendler, J., Lieberman H. and Wahlster W. (eds), *Spinning the Semantic Web: bringing the worldwide web to its full potential*, MIT Press.

Campbell, G. (2004) The Metadata-bibliographic Organization Nexus. In Gorman, G. E. and Dorner, D. G. (eds) *Metadata Applications and Management: International Yearbook of Library and Information Management 2003–2004*, Facet Publishing.

Chowdhury, G. G. (2004) *Introduction to Modern Information Retrieval*, Facet Publishing.

Dublin Core Metadata Initiative (2006) *Making it Easier to Find Information*, http://dublincore.org/.

Gorman, G. E. and Dorner, D. G. (eds) (2004) *Metadata Applications and Management: International Yearbook of Library and Information Management 2003–2004*, Facet Publishing.

Haynes, D. (2004) *Metadata: for information management and retrieval*, Facet Publishing.

Rasmussen, E. (2002) Indexing and Retrieval for the Web. In Cronin, B. (ed.) *ARIST* (Annual Review of Information Science and Technology), **37**, Information Today Inc.

# 8
# Metadata

## Introduction

Libraries have long been using mechanisms for creating 'surrogates' of bibliographic information resources that are used for resource discovery and information management; these are now termed 'metadata'. Library catalogues and bibliographies are good examples of metadata records. In order to create such metadata, libraries have prepared and adopted various standards like AACR2, MARC 21, etc. However, there is more to metadata than simple catalogue records or bibliographies. The term has long been used in the database world, and recently became popular in the information world in the context of handling and managing electronic information resources. In the context of the web, metadata play a number of key roles, ranging from resource discovery to information access, retrieval, sharing, processing, re-use, etc. Several metadata standards have been developed for handling specific types of information resources. This chapter begins with a discussion of the concept of metadata, its various types and its role in the organization and management of electronic information. It then analyses the basic needs and attributes required for metadata standards; this is followed by a description of the features and characteristics of certain metadata standards designed with a specific purpose in mind: the DCMI (Dublin Core Metadata Initiative) for bibliographic records, eGMS (e-Goverment Metadata Standard) for electronic government records, and ISAD(G) (General International Standard Archival Description) and EAD (Encoded Archival Description) for archival records. The chapter ends with a discussion of the management issues related to metadata.

## Metadata: what?

Metadata have been in existence since the first library catalogues were established over 2000 years ago in Alexandria in ancient Egypt. However, the term 'metadata' did not appear until the 1960s; it became established in the field of database management in the 1970s, and began to appear in the library and information science literature in the mid-1990s (Haynes, 2004; Lange and Winkler, 1997; Schwartz, 2001; Smiraglia, 2005; Vellucci, 1998).

Within a very short period of time, metadata became an important area of research and gave rise to many publications, including the *Annual Review of Information Science and Technology* (Vellucci, 1998) and a volume of the *International Yearbook of Library and Information Management* (Gorman and Dorner, 2004). Vellucci (1998) notes that the term transcends boundaries among various stakeholders in the internet arena, and provides a common vocabulary to describe a variety of data structures.

Simply speaking, metadata are data about data, but this definition does not say much about its purpose. There are several definitions of metadata in the literature. For example:

- Metadata describe various attributes of a resource (Dempsey and Heery, 1997).
- Metadata describe a discrete data object (Gill, 1998).
- Metadata provide users with some useful knowledge about the existence of records and their characteristics (Dempsey and Heery, 1998).
- Metadata describe the content, format and/or attributes of an information resource (Haynes, 2004).

Thus the term  metadata' describes the various attributes of a resource that are deemed useful to access, retrieve and manage it. According to UKOLN (the UK Office for Library Networking), University of Bath, it is normally understood to mean structured data about digital (and non-digital) resources that can be used to help support a wide range of operations, such as resource description, discovery, management (including rights management) and long-term preservation (UKOLN, n.d.). However, definitions of metadata vary depending on one's objectives and perspectives (Gilliand-Swetland, 1998, 2004). For example, for music resources usage is the most important determining factor for metadata. Music resources are used for several purposes – recreational listening, study, rehearsal, performance, etc. – and each purpose calls for a particular presentation layout, physical format and specific details (Vellucci, 2004).

## Metadata: why?

From the definitions of metadata discussed above, it may be concluded that metadata are created in order to add value to a resource in order to facilitate its discovery, use, sharing and re-use. The users of metadata are not only human beings; computer programs are becoming the main users of metadata. Metadata are important, both for information service providers and for the users of information services. Appropriate information modelling and metadata help service providers develop more effective information systems, and thus better information services, while an understanding of how metadata work helps users – especially specialist users – in a number of ways, such as improving their search for and use of information resources.

Libraries have long created catalogue records, as metadata, of their collections, which have been used by library users as well as librarians for a variety of purposes, particularly searching and retrieval of records. Catalogue records consist of item-specific information, and headings, etc. that have associated rules for further processing, such as rules for filing, etc. In today's world, however, while the term 'metadata' does not exclude non-electronic data, it is mostly applied to data in electronic form.

Haynes (2004) emphasizes that metadata can be used to describe electronic resources and digital data including image and multimedia resources, as well as printed resources such as books, journals and reports. Vellucci (1998) comments that the primary function of metadata is to facilitate the identification, location, retrieval, manipulation and use of digital objects in a networked environment. Duff and McKemmish (2000) report that in a metadata recordkeeping project in Australia eight purposes of metadata were identified. They can be used:

- to facilitate identification of resources
- for authentication of resources
- to ensure persistence of resources' content
- to provide structure and context of resources
- to store information relating to the administration of terms and conditions for access to, and disposal of, resources
- to facilitate the tracking and documenting of the history of resource use
- to assist users in the discovery, retrieval and delivery of resources
- to facilitate interoperability in a networked environment.

So, metadata serve a number of purposes for the user as well as for the information manager. Haynes (2004) proposes a five-point model that quite comprehensively describes the various roles played by metadata in managing electronic information. He proposes that metadata primarily serve the following five functions:

- Resource description: metadata facilitate the proper description and cataloguing of information resources, especially electronic and web resources.
- Information retrieval: metadata facilitate information retrieval, and several subject gateways use metadata for resource discovery and information retrieval.
- Management of information resources: metadata are the main building blocks of information architecture and content management, two newly developed fields within information services that aim to organize information in more effective ways so that it can be retrieved by users easily and intuitively.
- Determination of document ownership and authenticity of digital resources: metadata store important information about electronic information resources that can tell users about ownership, provenance, special marks, etc., which can be very useful for resource discovery and management.
- Ensuring interoperability and data transfer between systems: metadata formats enable data transfer between systems.

## Metadata: types

Metadata standards have been created by several communities dealing with information in some form or the other. The library world, for example, has developed the MARC formats as a means of encoding metadata, and has also defined descriptive standards in the ISBD (International Standard Bibliographic Description) series. The computing and web worlds have developed metadata standards based on implementations of the SGML (standard generalized markup language) or the XML (extensible markup language), examples being the EAD (encoded archival description) and the DTD (document type definition) (Day, 2001).

Dempsey and Heery (1998) have identified three groups of metadata:

1 Proprietary formats used by web indexing and search services: data are gathered by computer programmes and automatic records are created which are typically searched using the basic HTTP protocol.
2 Formats used for resource description: examples are Dublin Core and the ROADS (Resource Organization And Discovery in Subject-based services) templates. 'ROADS templates are used by the subject services which use the ROADS software. The templates are a development of the IAFA (Internet Anonymous FTP Archive) templates outlined in an IETF Internet Draft in 1994' (Day, 1997). Services that use this type of format include the OCLC's NetFirst and subject gateways created under the eLib programme.
3 Formats used for location, analysis, evaluation, documentation, etc. These formats are more complex and detailed, and specialist knowledge is required to create and maintain them. They may also be domain-specific. Examples are MARC, the FGDC's (Federal Geographic Data Committee's) content standard for digital geospatial metadata, the TEI (Text Encoding Initiative), EAD (Encoded Archival Description) and the ICPSR (Inter-university Consortium for Political and Social Research) initiative.

Mitchell and Surratt (2005) also categorize metadata into three groups but their discussion is based on the nature and purpose of the metadata:

- Structural metadata define logical or physical relationships among various parts of an information object.
- Descriptive metadata define the bibliographic features of information objects.
- Administrative metadata define information relevant to the creation, management and preservation of digital objects.

As discussed in the previous section, metadata are used to support specific activities, and hence we can classify metadata on the basis of their five major uses (Gilliand-Swetland, 1998):

- Administrative metadata which are used in managing and administering information resources.

- Descriptive metadata which are used to describe or identify information resources.
- Preservation metadata which are designed to specify the preservation management of information resources.
- Technical metadata which are used to describe how a system functions or how metadata behave.
- Use metadata which specify the level and types of use of information resources.

## Metadata standards

With the development of the internet and digital libraries, there has been increasing awareness of the need for metadata for the diverse categories of items available in digital form. Subject experts have developed, or are engaged in developing, various metadata formats for materials in specific domains, or for materials of specific kinds and formats: for example, metadata for internet resources, museum objects, government documents, archival records, etc. There are two distinct schools of thought that influence the development of metadata standards (Weibel, Iannella and Cathro, 1997):

- the minimalists' camp, whose point of view reflects a strong commitment to keeping metadata simple for the benefit of both document authors and tools that seek to use the metadata
- the structuralists' camp, whose members advocate greater flexibility in the formal metadata standards, so that metadata can be made more useful for the needs of a particular community.

Metadata standards have been written by experts in different subject areas, who have obviously come from different domains and understand information resources, users and their usage behaviour, and the overall requirements for resource discovery and description as they relate to their specific domains. Some of these metadata formats (MARC 21, Dublin Core, etc.) are general in nature and can accommodate descriptive information about digital information resources of different types in different disciplines, while others, such as the FGDC's content standard for digital geospatial metadata (FGDC, 2007) and the ISAD(G) (General International Standard Archival Description) for archival records

(International Council on Archives, 2000), are more specialized and apply to information in a specific discipline or domain (Vellucci, 1998).

## Dublin Core

The Dublin Core Metadata Initiative began in 1995 with an invitational workshop which brought together librarians, digital library researchers, content experts and text markup experts to develop discovery standards for electronic resources. The first meeting took place in Dublin, Ohio, and gave rise to a metadata format called the Dublin Core. Table 8.1 shows the 15 Dublin Core (DC) data elements (Dublin Core Metadata Initiative, 2006a, 2006b; also published as ISO Standard 15836:2003).

**Table 8.1** Dublin Core data elements

| Group | Element | Description |
|---|---|---|
| Content | Title | Name of the resource |
| | Subject | Topic describing the content of the resource |
| | Description | About the content of the resource |
| | Type | The nature or genre of the content of the resource |
| | Source | A reference to a resource from which the present resource is derived |
| | Relation | A reference to a related resource |
| | Coverage | The extent or scope of the content of the resource |
| Intellectual property | Creator | Who is primarily responsible for creating the content of the resource |
| | Publisher | Who is responsible for making the resource available |
| | Contributor | Who makes contributions to the content of the resource |
| | Rights | Information about rights held in and over the resource |
| Instantiation | Date | Date associated with the resource |
| | Format | The physical or digital manifestation of the resource |
| | Identifier | A unique reference to the resource within a given context |
| | Language | The language of the intellectual content of the resource |

The elements fall into three main groups which roughly indicate the class or scope of information stored in them: elements related mainly to the content of the resource, elements related mainly to the resource when it is viewed as an intellectual property and elements related mainly to the instantiation of the resource (Dublin Core Metadata Initiative, 2006b; Weibel, 1995; Weibel et al., 1998).

The Dublin Core Metadata Editor (DCDot, 2000) is a service that will retrieve a web page and automatically generate some Dublin Core metadata for it, suitable for embedding at the head (in the <head>...</head> section) of the page. In addition to generating instantly some DC tags for the webpage, the DCDot service also provides an editor to enable users to edit the tags or add to edit contents.

Figure 8.1 shows the DC metadata for a sample webpage. Dublin Core standard has the following characteristics (Taylor, 1999):

- The core set can be extended with further elements, as necessary, for a particular domain.
- All elements are optional.

```
<link rel="schema.DC" href="http://purl.org/dc">
<meta name="DC.Title" content="Gobinda Gopal Chowdhury">
<meta name="DC.Creator" content="Gobinda Chowdhury">
<meta name="DC.Subject" content="Gobinda Gopal Chowdhury;
Department of Computer and Information Sciences; University
of Strathclyde">
<meta name="DC.Description" content="Personal webpage">
<meta name="DC.Publisher" content="University of Strathclyde">
<meta name="DC.Contributor" content="Sudatta Chowdhury">
<meta name="DC.Date" content="31/01/2002">
<meta name="DC.Type" scheme="DCMIType" content="Text">
<meta name="DC.Format" content="text/html 10377 bytes">
<meta name="DC.Identifier" content=
"http://www.dis.strath.ac.uk/people/gobinda">
<meta name="DC.Source" content="Personal files">
<meta name="DC.Language" content="English">
<meta name="DC.Relation"
content="http://www.cis.strath.ac.uk;
http://www.strath.ac.uk">
<meta name="DC.Coverage" content="Brief CV and
Publications">
<meta name="DC.Rights" content="Gobinda Chowdhury">
```

**Figure 8.1** DC metadata for a sample web page

■ All elements are repeatable.
■ Any element can be modified by a qualifier.

## Other metadata standards

Several other metadata standards have been developed over the past few years to deal with specific types of digital resource. Dempsey (1996) describes some metadata and resource discovery initiatives in the UK's Electronic Libraries Programme (eLib) and within the European Union's Framework Programme for research and technological development. Dempsey and Heery (1997) provide an excellent review of several metadata standards, while Cromwell-Kessler (2000) maps several metadata standards to one another. The 2003 issue of the *International Yearbook of Library and Information Management* (Gorman and Dorner, 2004) provides an excellent account of metadata standards and developments in several fields, ranging from bibliographic and preservation activities to the fields of geospatial information, government information, music, art and education. Some metadata standards are briefly discussed in the following sections.

## e-GMS

e-GMS stands for e-Government Metadata Standard. It lays down the elements, refinements and encoding schemes to be used by UK government staff when creating metadata for information resources. It provides the core set of elements required to contain the data needed for the effective retrieval and management of government information (e-GMS, 2004). The e-GMS standard was designed to encourage people in government offices to use standard metadata sets to tag records in order to facilitate the easy discovery of, access to, management of and sharing of electronic information resources. Although it prescribes standard data elements, the e-GMS is flexible enough to allow the use of additional free text fields. Each element in e-GMS has a specific level of obligation, such as:

■ mandatory (this element must have a value for every resource)
■ mandatory, if applicable (this element must be given a value if applicable to the given resource)

- recommended (this element should be given a value if the data is available and appropriate to the given resource)
- optional (this element may be given a value if the data is available and appropriate to the given resource).

The data elements of e-GMS and their characteristics are listed in Table 8.2.

## ISAD(G) and EAD

The International Council on Archives has developed a general international standard for archival description, called ISAD(G) (International Council on Archives, 2000). The standard prescribes 26 data elements that can be used for describing archival materials. These 26 data elements are divided into seven groups:

- identity statement
- context
- content and structure
- conditions of access and use
- allied materials
- notes
- description control.

Although all the data elements are not mandatory, together they are considered essential in the exchange of archival data (International Council on Archives, 2000).

The EAD (Encoded Archival Description) is a metadata standard maintained jointly by the Library of Congress and the Society of American Archivists. It has a similar role in archival records as MARC has in bibliographic records. It defines structural elements and designates the content of descriptive guides to archival and manuscript holdings (Library of Congress, 2006). It is used internationally in an increasing number of archives and manuscript libraries to encode data describing corporate records and personal papers (Pitti, 1999).

From its inception, EAD was based on SGML, and from the release of EAD version 1.0 in 1998 it has also been compliant with XML. The latest version is EAD 2002 (Library of Congress, 2006). EAD 2002 provides a

## Table 8.2 Elements of the e-GMS metadata standard (e-GMS, 2004)

| Element | Description | Obligation |
|---|---|---|
| Accessibility | Denotes the resource's availability to specific groups; it enables users to limit their search to items they wish to access | Mandatory, if applicable |
| Addressee | Denotes the person(s) to whom the resource was addressed; it enables the user to identify the person(s) to whom the resource was dispatched | Optional |
| Aggregation | Denotes the resource's level or position in a hierarchy; it allows searches to be restricted to resources at a particular level | Optional |
| Audience | A category of user for whom the resource is intended; it enables the user to indicate the level or focus of the resource, and also enables filtering of a search to items suited to the intended audience | Optional |
| Contributor | Denotes the entity responsible for making contributions to the content of the resource; it enables users to retrieve a resource which has been contributed to by a particular person or organization | Optional |
| Coverage | Denotes the extent or scope of the content of the resource; it enables the user to limit the search according to the coverage | Recommended |
| Creator | Denotes the entity primarily responsible for making the content of the resource; it enables the user to find resources written or prepared by a particular individual or organization | Mandatory |
| Date | Denotes the date associated with an event in the life cycle of the resource; it enables the user to limit a search by date. | Mandatory |
| Description | Describes the content of the resource; it helps the users decide if the resource fits their needs | |
| Digital signature | Denotes a specific mark of the creator; it helps to decide the authenticity and ownership of the resource | Optional |
| Disposal | Accommodates the retention and disposal instructions for the resource; it helps in the management of resources | Optional |
| Format | Denotes the physical or digital manifestation of the resource; it allows the user to search for items of a particular format | Optional |

## Table 8.2 (continued)

| Element | Description | Obligation |
|---|---|---|
| Identifier | Provides an unambiguous reference to the resource within a given context; it allows the user to search for a specific version of a resource | Mandatory if applicable |
| Language | Denotes the language of the resource; it enables the user to limit a search by language | Recommended |
| Location | Denotes the physical location of the resource; it enables the user to locate the resource | Optional |
| Mandate | Denotes the legislative or other mandate under which the resource was produced; it helps the user understand and decide how to make use of the resource | Optional |
| Preservation | Provides for information to support the long-term preservation of a resource; it enables the organization make a decision about the preservation of the resource | Optional |
| Publisher | Denotes an entity responsible for making the resource available; it enables users to find a resource by a specific publisher | Mandatory if applicable |
| Relation | Denotes a reference to a related resource; it enables the user to find related resources | Optional |
| Rights | Used to store information about rights held in and over the resource; it indicates who has the rights to see, copy, redistribute, republish or otherwise make use of all or part of the resource | Optional |
| Source | Provides a reference to a resource from which the present resource is derived; it enables the user to find resources that have been developed using the content of a particular resource | Optional |
| Status | Denotes the position or state of the resource; it enables the user to search for resources of a particular status | Optional |
| Subject | Denotes the content of the resource; it enables the user to search by subject | Mandatory |
| Title | Denotes the title of the resource; it enables the user to find a resource with a particular title | Mandatory |
| Type | Denotes the nature or genre of the content of the resource; it enables the user to find a particular type of resource | Optional |

list of 146 data elements that may be used for the coding and exchange of archival information, such as: <abbr>—Abbreviation, —Abstract, <accessrestrict>—Conditions Governing Access, <acqinfo> —Acquisition Information, <archdesc>—Archival Description, <author> —Author, <bibref>—Bibliographic Reference, <custodhist>—Custodial History, <edition>—Edition, etc.

## TEI

The TEI (Text Encoding Initiative) was founded in 1987 to develop guidelines for encoding machine-readable texts in the humanities and social sciences. *TEI Guidelines for Electronic Text Encoding and Interchange* were first published in 1994 (www.tei-c.org/guidelines2/). These guidelines specify a set of tags which may be inserted to mark the text structure and other textual features of interest. TEIP4 appeared in print in June 2002, and the most recent release of TEIP5 appeared in 2006. The TEI guidelines enable the creation of many customized schemas (www.tei-c.org/guidelines2/).

## Metadata management

Metadata can be embedded within the information resources themselves, as is the case with web resources, or can be held separately in a database. Although metadata play an important role in the resource discovery process, end users don't see, and in most cases don't need to see, the metadata for the information resources that they are looking for. Metadata are mostly seen and used by information professionals who are involved in the organization and processing and information, and are used by computer programmes for purposes such as resource identification, sharing, interoperability, etc.

During the exchange and sharing of information resources between systems, consistency of metadata becomes an important issue. Consistency can be ensured in one of two ways:

■ through normalization of data available from various sources, but this may result in having to use the least specific data available; in other words, this will lead to the use of those metadata elements that are common to the resources available from various sources

■ by forcing every system to use the same metadata standard, although this may lead to several problems; agencies dealing with different sets of data and users may have to use different metadata standards, and also forced standardization may hinder innovation.

Metadata systems differ in terms of content and structure (Cromwell-Kessler, 2000). Content will differ if the rules that govern it differs. Different metadata standards create an obvious problem of interoperability. Each metadata system may comprise diverse data elements functioning at different levels. A simpler means of integration may be to translate one system to another as necessary. UKOLN and OCLC jointly organized a conference in 1996 to examine various general metadata issues and the Dublin Core metadata in particular. The meeting took place in Warwick, and gave rise to a new proposal called the Warwick framework (Dempsey and Weibel, 1996). While there was a consensus among the participants that the concept of a simple metadata set is useful, there was a fundamental question as to whether the Dublin Core really can be used for all types of digital document. It was agreed that a higher-level context for the Dublin Core has to be formulated which should define how it can be combined with other sets of metadata in a manner that addresses the individual integrity, distinct audiences and separate realms of responsibility of various distinct metadata sets. The Warwick Framework is a container architecture – a mechanism for aggregating logically, and perhaps physically, distinct packages of metadata (Lagoze, 1996).

The METS (Metadata Encoding and Transmission Standard), facilitates the interchange of metadata between digital libraries. It is designed to encode metadata for electronic texts, still images, digitized video, sound files and other materials within digital libraries (Gartner, 2002; METS, 2006).

## Summary

Metadata have become important in information organization since the advent of the internet. In this chapter we have discussed the concept of metadata and their importance in information handling and management. As discussed in this chapter, several metadata standards have been developed over the past few years. These standards each propose a set of data elements and an encoding scheme for the creation of metadata for specific types of information resources. Metadata standards play a number of roles in information organization and management: resource discovery, information retrieval, content management, information access control and management, re-use, etc. Metadata also play a key role in the management of intranet and web resources (Gill, 1998). The management of metadata is an important issue and, owing to the existence and use of several metadata standards, metadata interchange formats have had to be developed for sharing resources.

Metadata can play an important role in internet-based activities such as e-commerce, and in building the semantic web (see Chapter 12). Haynes (2004) comments that metadata are used for retrieval and interoperability among various systems, and thus can facilitate e-commerce transactions. Metadata can also play several roles in managing web information resources, such as ensuring rights management, the provenance of an item and intellectual property rights.

## REVIEW QUESTIONS

1 What are metadata and what role do they play in the organization of information?
2 What are the major functions of a metadata standard?
3 What is the Dublin Core and what is it used for?
4 What is e-GMS and what is it used for?
5 What are the various issues related to the management of metadata?

## References

Cromwell-Kessler, W. (2000) Crosswalks, Metadata Mapping, and Interoperability: what does it all mean? In Baca, M. (ed.), *Introduction to Metadata: pathways to digital information*, Getty Information Institute.

Day, M. (1997) *Interoperability Between Metadata Formats: mapping Dublin Core to ROADS templates*, www.ukoln.ac.uk/metadata/interoperability/dc_iafa.html.

Day, M. (2001) Metadata in a Nutshell, *Information Europe*, **6** (2), www.ukoln.ac.uk/metadata/publications/nutshell/.

DCDot (2000) Dublin Core Metadata Editor, www.ukoln.ac.uk/metadata/dcdot/.

Dempsey, L. (1996) ROADS to Desire: some UK and other European metadata and resource discovery projects, *D-Lib Magazine*, **2**, (July/August), www.dlib.org/dlib/july96/07dempsey.html.

Dempsey, L. and Heery, R. (1997) *A Review of Metadata: a survey of the current resource description formats* (work package 3 of telematics for research project DESIRE), www.ukoln.ac.uk/metadata/desire/overview.

Dempsey, L. and Heery, R. (1998) Metadata: a current view of practice and issues, *Journal of Documentation*, **54** (2), 145–72.

Dempsey, L. and Weibel, S. L. (1996) The Warwick Metadata Workshop: a framework for the deployment of resource description, *D-Lib Magazine*, 2, (July/August), http://dlib.ukoln.ac.uk/dlib/july96/07weibel.html.

Dublin Core Metadata Initiative (2006a) *Making it Easier to Find Information*, http://dublincore.org/.

Dublin Core Metadata Initiative (2006b) *Dublin Core Metadata Element Set, Version 1.1*, http://dublincore.org/documents/dces/.

Duff, W. and McKemmish, S. (2000) Metadata and ISO 9000 Compliance, *Information Management Journal*, **34** (1), www.sims.monash.edu.au/research/rcrg/publications/smckduff.html.

e-GMS (2004) *e-Government Metadata Standard Version 3.0*, www.esd.org.uk/standards/egms/.

FGDC (2007) *Geospatial metadata standards*, Federal Geographic Data Committee, www.fgdc.gov/metadata/geospatial-metadata-standards.

Gartner, G. (2002) *METS: Metadata Encoding and Transmission Standard*, www.jisc.ac.uk/index.cfm?name=techwatch_report_0205.

Gill, T. (1998) Metadata and the World Wide Web. In Baca, M. (ed.), *Introduction to Metadata: pathways to digital information*, Getty Information Institute.

Gilliand-Swetland, A. (1998) Defining Metadata. In Baca, M. (ed.), *Introduction to Metadata: pathways to digital information*, Getty Information Institute.

Gilliand-Swetland, A. (2004) Metadata: where are we going? In Gorman, G. E. and Dorner, D. G. (eds), *Metadata Applications and Management: International Yearbook of Library and Information Management 2003–2004*, Facet Publishing.

Gorman, G. E. and Dorner, D. G. (eds) (2004) *Metadata Applications and Management: International Yearbook of Library and Information Management 2003–2004*, Facet Publishing.

Haynes, D. (2004) *Metadata for Information Management and Retrieval*, Facet Publishing.

International Council on Archives (2000) *General International Standard Archival Description*, 2nd edn, International Council on Archives.

ISO Standard 15836:2003 *Information and Documentation: the Dublin Core metadata element set*, International Standards Organization.

Lagoze, C. (1996) The Warwick Framework: a container architecture for diverse sets of metadata, *D-Lib Magazine*, **2**, (July/August), www.dlib.org/dlib/july96/lagoze/07lagoze.html.

Lange, H. R. and Winkler, B. J. (1997) Taming the Internet: metadata, a work in progress. In Gordon, I. (ed.), *Advances in Librarianship*, Vol. 21, Academic Press.

Library of Congress (2006) *EAD: Encoded Archival Description. Version 2002*, www.loc.gov/ead/.

METS (2006) *Metadata Encoding and Transmission Standard*, www.loc.gov/standards/mets/.

Mitchell, A. and Surratt, B. E. (2005) *Cataloguing and Organizing Digital Resources*, Facet Publishing.

Pitti, D. V. (1999) Encoded Archival Description: an introduction and overview, *D-Lib Magazine*, **5** (11), www.dlib.org/dlib/november99/11pitti.html.

Schwartz, C. (2001) *Sorting Out the Web: approaches to subject access*, Ablex Publishing.

Smiraglia, R. P. (2005) Introducing Metadata, *Cataloguing and Classification Quarterly*, **40** (3/4), 1–15.

Taylor, A. (1999) *The Organization of Information*, Libraries Unlimited Inc.

UKOLN (n.d.) *Metadata*, www.ukoln.ac.uk/metadata/.

Vellucci, S. L. (1998) Metadata. In Williams, M. (ed.), *Annual Review of Information Science and Technology*, Vol. 33, Information Today Inc.

Weibel, S. (1995) Metadata: the foundations of resource description, *D-Lib Magazine*, **1**, (July), www.dlib.org/dlib/july95/07weibel.html.

Weibel, S., Iannella, R. and Cathro, W. (1997) The 4th Dublin Core Metadata Workshop Report. DC4, March 3–5, National Library of Australia, Canberra, *D-Lib Magazine*, **3**, (June), www.dlib.org/dlib/june97/metadata/06weibel.html.

Weibel, S., Kunze, J., Lagoze, C. and Wolf, M. (1998) *Network Working Group Request for Comments: 2413*, www.ietf.org/rfc/rfc2413.txt.

# 9
# Markup languages

## Introduction

For computers to recognize and process data from a variety of information resources automatically, in a machine- and software-independent manner, a common language must be used for marking various sections of information resources. Markup languages are used for this purpose. Several markup languages have been developed over the years, and although they may have some similarities, or may have the same origin, they are each designed to meet a different purpose; overall each markup language plays a particular key role in the organization and processing of electronic information. This chapter begins with a brief outline of SGML (Standard Generalized Markup Language), which formed the basis of other markup languages. It then discusses the nature and characteristics of the two best known and most widely used families of markup languages, HTML (HyperText Markup Language) and XML (eXtensible Markup Language), together with their related schema DTD (document type definition) and XML. Applications of XML and related technologies like RDF are dealt with in Chapter 12.

## SGML

Markup languages are designed to mark specific sections of information resources with standard codes or tags, which are interpreted by computer programs as instructions to take specific measures, for example to display text appropriately (e.g. in bold or in colour), or to extract a specific portion of the item (e.g. title, keywords, abstract, etc.) into a database for storage or into a file for further processing.

SGML, the Standard Generalized Markup Language, as the name suggests, is a language for marking up text documents so that they can be processed by computer independently of any software and hardware differences. It was accepted as an international standard in 1986 (ISO 8879:1986). SGML was created to provide a set of rules that describe the structure of an electronic document so that it may be interchanged across various computer platforms. SGML also allows users to:

- link files together to form composite documents
- identify where illustrations are to be incorporated into text files
- create different versions of a document in a single file
- add editorial comments to a file
- provide information to supporting programmes.

To allow the computer to do as much of the work as possible, SGML requires the user to provide a model of the document being produced. This model, called a DTD (document type definition), describes each element of the document and formally identifies the relationships between its various elements.

SGML defines data in terms of elements and attributes. A particular unit of an item – its title, abstract, section heading, etc. – is considered an element. An attribute gives particular information about an element. SGML uses tags and delimiters to mark-up different elements. For example, the author of a text may be marked as <author> Gobinda G. Chowdhury </author>. In this example, the author name is marked by <author>; the element between <and> signs (here, author) denotes the content (here, the author's name). The end of an element is denoted by the tag name preceded by '/'. SGML provides an extensive list of tags and supports many variations of them. An SGML document consists of three parts (Schwartz, 2001):

- the SGML declaration defining the document character set, name lengths for elements and other basic parameters
- the DTD
- the document instance – i.e. the actual document.

SGML has been used widely in the publishing community, and has given rise to several other markup languages and other applications such as HTML (HyperText Markup Language) and XML (eXtensible Markup Language), as well as TEI (the Text Encoding Initiative) and EAD (Encoded Archival Description).

## HTML

SGML provides an extensive mechanism for marking up electronic documents, but it does have some problems. The process of marking up a text using SGML is fairly complex and resource-intensive. A simpler markup language called HTML (HyperText Markup Language) developed by Tim Berners-Lee quickly became the primary language for preparing web documents. It contains a set of markup symbols or codes that are inserted into a file intended for display on a browser page. The HTML markup tells the web browser how to display the web page's content – text, image, etc. – for the user. Each individual markup code is referred to as an element or a tag. Some elements come in pairs and indicate when a display effect is to begin and when it is to end. HTML is formally recommended by the W3C (World Wide Web Consortium) and is generally adhered to by the major browsers like Internet Explorer and Netscape Navigator. Information about HTML, including the specifications, guidelines for use, etc., is available on the W3C website (W3C, 2006).

An HTML tag is a code element that appears as letters or words between a < and a >. For example <title>. To tell the web browser to end doing what it has just been asked to do (for example, to tell the browser where the title ends), a forward slash is used in the closing tag: </title>. Most tags come in matched 'beginning' and 'ending' pairs, but this is not an absolute rule. Any web page will contain the following tags at the start of the page:

- <HTML>: tells the web browser that this is the beginning of an HTML document
- <HEAD>: tells that web browser that this is the header for the page
- <TITLE>: tells the web browser that this is the title of the page
- <BODY>: tells the web browser that this is the beginning of the web page's content.

HTML soon became the *lingua franca* for publishing documents on the web. It is a non-proprietary format based on SGML, and can be created and processed by a wide range of tools, from simple plain text editors – where all content, including codes, is typed in from scratch – to sophisticated editing tools like Microsoft Frontpage. HTML has a wide range of features reflecting the needs of a very diverse and international community wishing to make information available on the web.

Originally HTML was designed to facilitate the exchange of scientific and other technical documents, but be suitable for use by non-document specialists. Thus HTML addressed the problem of SGML complexity by specifying a small set of structural and semantic tags suitable for authoring relatively simple documents. In 1995, the W3C released version 2 of HTML, and the fourth and final version appeared in 1999, quickly followed by version 4.01, which fixed some of the problems in version 4. In addition to simplifying the document structure, HTML added support for hypertext and multimedia capabilities. Figure 9.1 shows some sample HTML codes, and Figure 9.2 shows the corresponding output.

```
<!DOCTYPE HTML PUBLIC "-//W3C//DTD HTML 4.0
Transitional//EN">
<!-- saved from url=(0037)http://www.cis.strath.ac.uk/
~gobinda/ -->
<HTML><HEAD><TITLE>Gobinda Gopal Chowdhury</TITLE>
<META http-equiv=Content-Type content="text/html;
charset=iso-8859-1">
<META content="Microsoft FrontPage 5.0" name=GENERATOR>
<META content=FrontPage.Editor.Document name=ProgId>
<META content="bars 011" name="Microsoft Theme"></HEAD>
<BODY>
<P align=center></B><B><FONT color=#800000 size="5">Welcome
to my home page </FONT></B></P>
<P align=center></P>
<P align=center><B><I><SPAN
style="COLOR: #cc0000; FONT-FAMILY: 'Viner Hand ITC';
mso-bidi-font-family: Arial">  Gobinda
Chowdhury</SPAN></I></B></P>
<P align=center><B><I><SPAN
style="COLOR: #cc0000; FONT-FAMILY: 'Viner Hand ITC';
mso-bidi-font-family: Arial">
University of Strathclyde, Glasgow</SPAN></I></B></P>
<p align="center"> </p>
</BODY></HTML>
```

**Figure 9.1** A simple HTML file

In a very short space of time, the simplicity of HTML made it popular. However, since its inception, there has been rapid invention of new elements – for use within standard HTML and for adapting HTML to specialized user requirements. This plethora of new elements has led to interoperability problems across different platforms. There are many

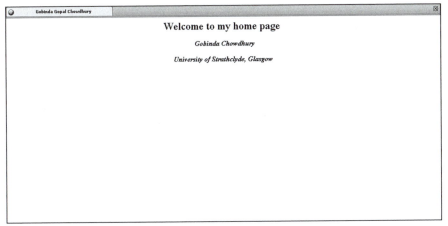

**Figure 9.2** Output of the HTML code shown in Figure 9.1

varieties of HTML, and software packages like Microsoft Frontpage use many non-standard codes, which makes them proprietary formats. Several programs, like Java and Perl, have been designed to work with HTML for information processing on the web, but not every browser always responds properly to these extended facilities.

In January 2000 the W3C brought out the XHTML 1.0 specification which, simply speaking, was HTML 4.01 reformulated to follow XML rules. Thus it is compatible with all XML-based languages. As stated in the specification (W3C, 2002), XHTML is a family of document types and modules that reproduce, act as a subset to, and extend HTML version 4; they are XML based and designed to work in conjunction with XML-based user agents.

## XML

### Origin and meaning

While SGML is too complex and resource-intensive to encode and cannot be processed as it is by web browsers, and HTML is too simple and only tells the browser how to present an element or how to link to another item, XML (eXtensible Markup Language) aims to offer the best of both the worlds. XML is a simple and flexible format derived from SGML. It contains a set of rules for designing text formats that lets users structure their data. Development of XML started in 1996 and it has been recommended by the W3C since February 1998. The third edition of version 1 of XML was published as a W3C recommendation in February 2004 (W3C, 2004a). The designers of XML simply took the best parts of SGML, guided by their experience with HTML, and produced something that is powerful and vastly more regular and simple to use. XML is a cross-platform, software- and hardware-independent tool for sharing machine-processable information.

## XML: what for?

XML is intended to allow computers to generate data, read data and ensure that the data structure is unambiguous. It is extensible and platform-independent, and it supports internationalization as well as localization. XML was conceived as a means of regaining the power and flexibility of SGML without most of its complexity. Thus XML preserves most of SGML's power and richness but removes many of the more complex features of SGML, and thus is an easy-to-use yet very effective tool.

XML is a metalanguage that meets the need to define application-specific markup tags (Ding et al., 2002). It is an ideal data format for storing structured and semi-structured text intended for dissemination and ultimate publication on a variety of media (Bradley, 2000). Originally designed to meet the challenges of large-scale electronic publishing, XML now plays an increasingly important role in the exchange of a wide variety of data over the web (W3C, 2004a).

XML establishes a set of rules for creating other languages. As long as a langauge follows the rules of XML, it is considered to be XML-compliant. An XML document contains tags which enclose identifiable parts of the document. An XML document has both a logical and a physical structure: the logical structure allows a document to be divided into units and sub-units, called elements, and the physical structure of the document allows entities – components of the document – to be stored separately in different files (Bradley, 2000).

## HTML vs XML

Both HTML and XML are markup languages; they allow us to publish content and provide information about what role the content plays.

However, there are certain differences. XML and HTML were designed with different goals in mind: while HTML was designed to display data and to focus on how data looks on the browser, XML was designed to describe data and to focus on specifying the nature of the enclosed data. HTML is about displaying information, while XML is about describing information.

While HTML specifies what each tag and attribute means, and often how the text between them should appear in a browser, XML uses tags only to delimit pieces of data, and leaves the interpretation of the data completely to the application that reads it. Like HTML, XML files are text files that people shouldn't have to read, but they may do so when the need arises. XML is a framework that allows users to produce application-specific codes, with markup, so that the tags become meaningful in terms of data and content, thus making the resultant XML documents suitable for machine-processing. However, unlike HTML, XML is not fault tolerant, and a forgotten tag or an attribute without quotes makes an XML file unusable.

## Characteristics of XML

XML was first developed by an XML working group under the auspices of the W3C in 1996. There were ten design goals for XML (W3C, 2004a). In essence, these state that XML should be easy to use and compatible with SGML, that the design of XML should be formal, with a minimal number of optional features, that it should be easy to create XML documents and that such documents should be clear, concise and readable.

XML has certain characteristics that distinguish it from HTML (Antoniou and van Harmelen, 2004; Sauers, 2004):

**1** Like HTML, XML uses tags, but unlike HTML all tags in XML must be closed. The enclosed content, together with its opening and closing tags, is called an element in XML.

**2** An HTML document cannot represent structural information (information about various pieces of a document and their precise relationships). In contrast, in an XML document specific parts or components of a document can be marked by user-defined vocabulary, and can be easily read and processed by computers.

**3** In HTML tags are specified and users cannot define them. In contrast, an XML representation can include user-defined tags, and they can be virtually anything. For example, the following brief XML statements have user-defined tags:

```
<book>
  <title>Introduction to digital libraries
  </title>
  <author>G. Chowdhury</author>
  <author>S. Chowdhury</author>
  <publisher>Facet Publishing</publisher>
  <Year>2003</year>
</book>
<equation>
  <meaning>Momentum equation</meaning>
  <leftside>Momentum</leftside>
  <rightside>Mass x velocity</rightside>
</equation>
```

Thus in XML one can use information in various ways, and it is up to the user to define a vocabulary that is suitable.

**4** Since vocabulary is important, and people in different domains use different terminologies, XML applications have been defined in various domains: MathML for mathematics, BSML for bioinformatics, HRML for human resources, AML for astronomy, newsML for news and IRML for investment.

**5** Companies and businesses often need to gather data from a range of sources, such as from customers and various commercial and non-commercial sources. XML can serve as a uniform data exchange format, and thus can facilitate such gathering, processing, re-use and distribution of data across various applications.

## XML documents

An XML document may consist of one or more units called entities, which contain character data and markup; each entity has some content and is identified by an entity name (W3C, 2004a, 2004b). XML documents can be created using standard text editors or specialized XML-sensitive editors.

An XML document consists of a prologue, elements and optionally an epilogue. A prologue consists of an XML declaration and an optional reference to external structuring documents. Elements in an XML document also constitute entities; they represent the things that the XML document is about, such as people, books, cars, etc. The content of each element is enclosed within opening and closing tags that are chosen by the document creator.

In every XML document there is one element which is called the root, no part of which appears in the content of any other element. For every other element, if the start tag is within the content of another element, then the end tag must also be within the content of the same element. In the formal W3C definition (2004a):

> [For] each non-root element C in the document, there is one other element P in the document such that C is in the content of P, but is not in the content of any other element that is in the content of P. P is referred to as the parent of C, and C as a child of P.

It should be noted that XML only provides a data format for documents. Unlike an HTML document, which contains standard tags that can be interpreted by computer programs as instructions for the display of the enclosed information, interpretation of the meaning of the tags in an XML document depends on the user and the application. XML does not imply a specific interpretation of the data. For example, the following two simple XML statements: <author><name>Gobinda Chowdhury</name></author> and <patient><name>Gobinda Chowdhury</name></patient> refer to the same person possibly in two different contexts. Human indexers can easily infer that in the first instance the person referred to is an author of a book or an article (or some sort of an artistic creation), while in the second the same person is considered as a patient (maybe in a hospital). However, when such information is passed to an application, the context and meaning of the tags should be known to that application in order for it to be able to process the data appropriately.

An XML document is said to be valid if it is well formed, and if it uses and conforms to structuring information. There are two standard ways of defining the structure of XML documents: by using DTDs, or by using the more advanced XML schema.

## DTDs

DTD stands for document type definition. As discussed in the previous section, XML allows us to encode all kinds of data structures and use almost any kind of vocabulary in the tags, but it does not specify the semantics and use of the data. The applications that use XML for data exchange must understand each other, and agree on the vocabulary, its meaning and use, and so on. A DTD or an XML schema is used to specify this vocabulary and to define the tags and their combinations.

A DTD defines the legal building blocks of an XML document; it defines the document structure with a list of legal elements. One can define a DTD inside an XML document, or one can give it as an external reference. However, it is better to use external DTDs, otherwise there may be duplication and it becomes difficult to maintain consistency (Antoniou and van Harmelen, 2004). If the DTD is external to the XML source file, it should be wrapped in a DOCTYPE definition. The following is an example of a declaration that refers to an external DTD:

```
<!DOCTYPE html PUBLIC "-//W3C//DTD XHTML 1.0
Transitional//EN" "www.w3.org/TR/xhtml1/DTD/
xhtml1-transitional.dtd<!DOCTYPE html">
```

Thus when using a DTD, each XML file can carry a description of its own format; therefore, an application can use a standard DTD to verify the data received from the outside world. A DTD can also help one verify one's own data.

## XML schema

Just like a DTD, an XML schema defines the legal building blocks of an XML document. It is therefore an alternative to a DTD for describing XML structure. It is intended to allow more expressive data validation than DTD. XML schemas provide uniqueness constraints and references, which denote specific attributes of the elements that make them unique and relate them to others. They support various data types and namespaces. An XML namespace is a collection of names, identified by a URI (uniform resource identifier), which are used in XML documents as element types and attribute names. An XML schema has some essential characteristics. For example, an XML schema defines (W3Schools, 2006):

- the elements that can appear in a document
- the attributes that can appear in a document
- which elements are child elements
- the order of child elements
- the number of child elements
- whether an element is empty or can include text
- the data types for elements and attributes
- the default and fixed values for elements and attributes.

The purpose of an XML schema is to define a class of XML documents; the term 'instance document' is often used to describe an XML document that conforms to a particular XML schema (W3Schools, 2006).

Figure 9.3 shows an example adapted from an XML schema shown at W3Schools (2006) called the purchase order schema. It uses XML version 1.0. The purchase order schema consists of one main element: purchaseOrder. It also contains four subelements: shipTo, billTo, comment and items. Each subelement in turn contains other subelements, or a

```
<?xml version="1.0"?>
<purchaseOrder orderDate="2006-10-20">
   <shipTo country="UK">
      <name>John Smith</name>
      <street>123 George Street</street>
      <city>Glasgow</city>
            <postcode>G1 3BU</zip>
   </shipTo>
   <billTo country="UK">
      <name>Robert Smith</name>
.......
   </billTo>
   <comment>Hurry ..........<!/comment>
   <items>
      <item partNum="872-AA">
         <productName>Cooker</productName>
         <quantity>1</quantity>
         <UKPrice>148.95</UKPrice>
         <comment>Confirm this is electric</comment>
      </item>
   ............
      </item>
   </items>
</purchaseOrder>
```

**Figure 9.3** Purchase order schema

number, as in the case of UKPrice. Elements that contain subelements or carry attributes are said to be complex types, whereas elements that contain numbers (and strings and dates, etc.) but do not contain any subelements are said to be simple types.

## Summary

Markup languages – especially HTML, which is the *lingua franca* of the web – have brought about a revolution in the information world. We use HTML to create every page on the web; one can use raw HTML codes or can use an editor that makes the job of coding much easier. While HTML ensures that data is displayed in the browser in the desired way, it does not support data processing, because HTML documents can only store and pass on style information, not the meaning or data processing information. XML was created as a new standard markup language for this purpose. XML, together with appropriate DTD or XML schema, enables computers to gather and process data easily. These, together with other technologies like RDF and URI, play a key role in building the semantic web, which is discussed in Chapter 12.

## REVIEW QUESTIONS

1 What is a markup language?
2 What are SGML and HTML?
3 What is XML?
4 What is the difference between HTML and XML?
5 What role is played by XML and related technologies in organizing and processing information?

## References

Antoniou, G. and van Harmelen, F. (2004) *A Semantic Web Primer*, MIT Press.
Bradley, N. (2000) *The XML Companion*, 2nd edn, Addison-Wesley.
Ding, Y., Fensel, D., Klein, M. C. A. and Omelayenko, B. (2002) The Semantic Web: yet another hip?, *Data & Knowledge Engineering*, **41** (2–3), 205–27.

ISO8879:1986 *Information Processing: text and office systems: standard generalized markup language (SGML)*, International Standards Organization.

Sauers, M. P. (2004) *XHTML and CSS Essentials for Library Web Design*, Neal-Schuman.

Schwartz, C. (2001) *Sorting out the Web: approaches to subject access*, Ablex Publishing.

W3C (2002) *XHTML™ 1.0 The Extensible HyperText Markup Language (Second Edition): a reformulation of HTML 4 in XML 1.0*, www.w3.org/tr/xhtml1/.

W3C (2004a) *Extensible Markup Language (XML) 1.0*, 3rd edn, www.w3.org/tr/2004/rec-xml-2004020.

W3C (2004b) *XML Schema Part 0: primer second edition*, Fallside, D. C. and Walmsley, P. (eds), www.w3.org/tr/xmlschema-0/.

W3C (2006) HyperText Markup Language (HTML), home page, www.w3.org/markup/.

W3Schools (2006) *Introduction to XML schema*, www.w3schools.com/schema/schema_intro.asp.

## Ontology: origin and meaning

The term 'ontology' originates from philosophy, where it is used to denote the branch of metaphysics that is concerned with, simply speaking, the kinds of things that exist and how to describe them. The origin of the term 'ontology' can be traced back to 1721, as an abstract philosophical notion (McGuinness, 2003). Over the past few years, the term has gained a new meaning and is used in several fields of study, including knowledge engineering, knowledge management, information retrieval and, more recently, the world wide web. Its generally accepted meaning in these fields is the specification of a conceptualization, as defined by Gruber (1993). Vickery was one of the first information scientist to draw attention to the term 'ontology', and in his 1997 paper he reviewed some of the more important ontologies of that time and reported on the thinking of the leaders in the field (Gilchrist, 2003).

There are several definitions of ontology; Guarino (1997) presents a good survey of them. The most widely used definition of ontology, in the context of information and knowledge management, appears to be the one proposed by Gruber (1993), which says that an ontology is a formal, explicit specification of a shared conceptualization. This definition highlights certain inherent characteristics of an ontology. The word 'conceptual-ization' in the definition refers to 'an abstract model of phenomena in the world by having identified the relevant concepts of those phenomena' (Ding and Foo, 2002a). The word 'explicit' in the definition of ontology suggests that the concepts used, as well as the constraints on their use, should be explicitly defined in an ontology. The word 'formal' in the definition of ontology suggests that an ontology should be based on formal logic in order to be machine-readable, and the word 'shared' indicates that an ontology should include agreed and shared notions of vocabulary – terms, their relationships, constraints, etc. – in a domain. Pidcock (2003) provides a simple definition of ontologies that includes mention of an ontology language, its underlying grammar and its role:

> A formal ontology is a controlled vocabulary expressed in an ontology representation language. This language has a grammar for using vocabulary terms to express something meaningful within a specified domain of interest. The grammar contains formal constraints (e.g. it specifies what it means to be a well-formed statement, assertion, query, etc.) on how terms in the ontology's controlled vocabulary can be used together.                              (Pidcock, 2003)

An ontology consists of a finite list of terms, representing concepts or classes of objects and their relationships (especially the hierarchical relationships), and providing other information such as properties, value restrictions, disjointness statements and specification of logical relationships between concepts (Antoniou and van Harmelen, 2004).

In the context of the web, ontologies provide a shared understanding of a domain that is necessary to understand differences in the connotations of terms, and thus to facilitate interoperability and data processing by computers.

## Ontology, taxonomy and thesauri

So, if an ontology consists of terms in a given domain and shows the relationships among them, their uses and their constraints, etc., how does it differ from tools like taxonomies and thesauri, which have long been used in organizing and processing information in the library and information world? Are there any real differences? Researchers have different opinions: some have pointed out differences, others say that these tools are not significantly different from one another.

A thesaurus is a networked collection of controlled vocabulary terms showing synonyms, hierarchical and other relationships, and dependencies. A thesaurus tells us the valid index terms in a given domain, and how a given term is related to other terms within the domain or the universe of knowledge. Thesauri have long been used as essential tools for indexing and searching for information.

A taxonomy, simply speaking, is some sort of classification of topics in a given domain that relates to its general laws and principles. A taxonomy is a collection of controlled vocabulary terms organized into a hierarchical structure; each term in a taxonomy is in one or more parent–child relationships with other terms in the taxonomy (Pidcock, 2003). Warner (2004) notes that, although the term 'taxonomy' originated in the scientific community, for example in biology to denote hierarchies of families of plants and animals, in the field of information science, especially in the context of information architecture (discussed in Chapter 11), the term may mean anything from simple lists and navigation hierarchies to thesauri.

Gilchrist commented in 2003 that the word 'taxonomy' was being used at that time with at least five separate meanings, although with some overlap:

- taxonomies in the form of web directories
- taxonomies created to support automatic indexing
- taxonomies created by automatic categorization
- front end filters, where a taxonomy is either created or imported and used in query formulation
- corporate taxonomies that are specifically built to make information easily accessible to staff through an enterprise information portal or other channel.

Gilchrist (2004) suggests that a taxonomy can be:

- a human-generated algorithm to support automatic indexing, where large inputs call for automatic indexing
- a categorization automatically produced by software
- a tool used on a search interface to provide support in query formulation
- a front-end navigation tool such as the Yahoo! Directory (http://dir.yahoo.com/) or the DMOZ Open Directory Project (http://dmoz.org/).

McGuinness (2003) suggests that glossaries, controlled vocabularies and thesauri are all simple forms of ontology, in that they all provide a list of terms and their relationships in a given domain. However, ontologies need to have certain additional characteristics that can be provided only through the use of formal logic. An ontology describes its subject matter using the notions of concepts, instances, relations, functions and axioms (Gilchrist, 2003).

Gilchrist (2003) provides a neat comparison of taxonomy, thesaurus and ontology. He comments that when looking at the applications of thesauri, taxonomies and ontologies, a progression of ideas can be noted. He further suggests:

> [T]he post-Roget thesaurus has been the domain of information scientists; taxonomies appear to have been generated by a combination of information technologists and systems developers in corporate businesses together with software vendors; and ontologies have been adapted from the work of philosophers by people working in artificial intelligence. (Gilchrist, 2003, 14–15)

Taxonomies, thesauri and ontologies all use natural language terms that are shared by, and agreed on within, a community.

## Some common examples of ontology

Ontologies can be simple or advanced and complex. Simple ontologies, that may be in the form of a taxonomy or a thesaurus, are easier and less expensive to build; many simple ontologies are available on the web, and many more have been built for use within organizations.

CYC is a registered trademark owned by Cycorp, Inc., in Austin, Texas, USA. The CYC knowledge base (www.cyc.com/cyc/technology/technology/whatiscyc_dir/ whatsincyc), containing nearly 200,000 terms and several dozen hand-entered assertions about each term, is a formalized representation of a vast amount of fundamental human knowledge: facts, rules of thumb and heuristics for reasoning about the objects and events of everyday life. Although the main CYC knowledge base is proprietary, a research version is available for free.

WordNet (http://wordnet.princeton.edu/), developed by the Cognitive Science Laboratory at Princeton University, USA, is another example of an ontology: English nouns, verbs, adjectives and adverbs are organized into synonym sets, each representing one underlying lexical concept. WordNet can be downloaded for free from the web.

The DMOZ Open Directory (www.dmoz.com) is another example of a simple ontology. It is one of the largest and most comprehensive human-edited directories, comprising over 590,000 categories constructed and maintained by over 71,000 volunteer editors.

In the biomedical sciences, the Unified Medical Language System (UMLS) of the US National Library of Medicine (www.nlm.nih.gov/research/umls/) is yet another example of a simple ontology. It is a large and sophisticated knowledge source comprising the Metathesaurus, the Semantic Network and the SPECIALIST lexicon. The Gene Ontology (www.geneontology.org/), first constructed in 1998, is a freely accessible ontology to facilitate access to gene products in different databases. OBO (Open Biomedical Ontologies) (http://obo.sourceforge.net/) provides access to a number of well-structured controlled vocabularies for shared use across different biological and medical domains. Ontologies that are accessible through the OBO site are listed in a table; the list is also arranged hierarchically and can be browsed.

Ontologies have been developed in various other disciplines: for example, ISO 21127 (2005) is a reference ontology for the interchange of cultural heritage information.

## Ontologies: what do they do?

McGuiness (2003) lists a number of mandatory, typical and desirable characteristics of ontologies. A simple ontology provides support for information organization and management activities. In addition, advanced ontologies have some further characteristics that provide further support for information management and sharing. The following are some important uses of ontology (McGuiness, 2003). It:

- provides a controlled vocabulary that can be used by humans as well as computers to access and manage information
- supports site organization and management
- supports expectation-setting, in that a quick look at an ontology may give the user an idea of what can be expected from a website
- may be used as an umbrella structure which may be used for further extension by individual applications with specific hierarchies of categories
- supports browsing and searching
- may be used to support sense disambiguation; if the same term appears in more than one place the corresponding class and subclass hierarchies may help the user/program distinguish between the various contexts of the term
- may be used for consistency checking, by using the properties of classes and/or their restrictions, etc.
- may be used to augment the information obtained by the user/application with other information from corresponding classes/subclasses/properties in the ontology
- provides support for interoperability among systems by using shared vocabulary, restrictions on values, etc.
- may be used to support validation and verification of data.

## Building an ontology: guidelines and methods

An ontology can be built from scratch, from an existing global or local ontology, from a corpus of information sources or from a combination of these approaches. The method can be manual or semi-automatic; however, fully automatic methods for building large-scale ontologies are rare. Several ontology design principles have been proposed by researchers. Ding and Foo (2002a, 2002b) have reviewed some of these principles:

- The formal ontology design approach proposed by Guarino, Masolo and Vetere (1999) has some basic principles, such as: the need for a clear understanding of the domain and the users, identification of a basic taxonomic structure and identification of the specific roles of users.
- The skeletal methodology proposed by Uschold and Gruninger (1996) suggests that after identifying the purpose and scope of the ontology, a five-step manual process may be followed: ontology capture (identification of important concepts, their relationships, etc.), ontology coding (choosing a representation language, writing the codes, integrating existing ontology, etc.), evaluation, documentation and then preparing guidelines for all of these previous stages.
- The ontological design patterns put forward by Jannink et al. (1998) involve identification of ontological design structures, terms, larger expressions and semantic contexts.

Denny (2004) suggests:

[A]n ontology building process may span problem specification, domain knowledge acquisition and analysis, conceptual design and commitment to community ontologies, iterative construction and testing, publishing the ontology as a terminology, and possibly populating a conforming knowledge base with ontology individuals.

In an earlier work, Denny (2002) proposed the following five steps for building an ontology:

- Acquire the domain knowledge: the first step is to assemble appropriate information resources and expertise, to define terms in the domain of interest; these definitions must be collected with consensus and consistency so that they can be expressed in a common language throughtout the ontology.
- Organize the ontology: the second step is to design the overall

conceptual structure of the domain, which will involve a number of activities, such as: identifying the domain's principal concrete concepts and their properties, identifying the relationships among the concepts, creating abstract concepts, referencing or including supporting ontologies, distinguishing which concepts have instances, etc.

- Flesh out the ontology: at this stage, concepts, relations and individual terms or elements are added to the level of detail necessary to satisfy the purposes of the ontology.
- Check your work: the next step is to reconcile any syntactic, logical and semantic inconsistencies among the ontology elements.
- Commit the ontology: finally, the ontology has to be verified by domain experts, which will follow the publishing and deployment of the ontology.

So, although the specific steps for building an ontology, as listed above, may differ, the basic knowledge required to build an ontology is always the same: an understanding of the domain, the people and the their tasks, and of the various taxonomies available in the given domain (if any).

## Tools for building an ontology

A number of tools, or ontology editors, are now available that can be used to build an ontology. Denny (2004) surveyed 94 ontology editors, compared their features and provided contact addresses for obtaining additional information, etc. Many ontology building tools and editors are available for free. For example, Protégé is a free ontology editor and knowledge acquisition system available from the Protégé website (http://protege. stanford.edu/). It was developed by Stanford Medical Informatics at the Stanford University School of Medicine, with support from a number of agencies in the USA. Currently it has over 41,500 users worldwide creating ontology and knowledge bases in different areas such as biomedicine, corporate modelling, intelligence gathering, e-learning, and so on. WebOnto (http://kmi.open.ac.uk/projects/webonto/) is another freely accessible tool that allows users to browse and edit knowledge models. A number of freely available tools have also been developed within the Gene Ontology Consortium (www.geneontology.org/GO.tools.shtml).

Choosing an appropriate ontology building tool is not a trivial task; a number of factors need to be considered (Denny, 2004):

- It is important to ensure that expressiveness is not lost and consistency is not compromised when moving between tools: it may be necessary to look for a common ontology specification and interchange language.
- When editors do not natively support OWL (Web Ontology Language, discussed below) import and export (from different ontology languages), specific translator tools should be identified to bridge the editor's native language(s) and OWL.
- Ontology tools can differ markedly in their level of use and maturity: choosing tools that have active development and user communities should ensure that the tools will continue to be available and kept up to date.
- It is also important to consider the level of technical support and training available from the software provider or the community supporting the tool.
- It is better to choose editors with a software architecture that allows easy extension – addition of functionality and integration with other tools, including common application frameworks, plug-in facilities, etc.
- It is important to be familiar with the licensing terms, purchase price or terms of reference, documentation, update policy and upgrade path.

## Ontology languages: DAML+OIL and OWL

In order to build an ontology we need a language. An ontology language should have:

- a well defined syntax – necessary for machine processing of information
- a formal semantics – a pre-requisite for reasoning support: it formally specifies class membership, equivalence of classes, consistency and classification
- convenience of expression
- efficient reasoning support
- sufficient expressive power.

A number of possible languages can be used, including general logic programming languages like Prolog. However, a number of special languages have evolved specifically to support ontology construction, the most common ones being he DAML+OIL and OWL. DAML stands for the DARPA Agent Markup Language (whose goal is to create technologies to enable software agents to identify and understand information sources, and to provide interoperability between agents), and OIL stands for Ontology Interchange Language. DAML+OIL is the joint name of the American DAML-ONT (DAML Ontology) and the European language OIL. DAML+OIL was taken as a starting point by the W3C Working Group on Web Ontology in defining OWL, the standard and broadly accepted ontology language of the semantic web (Antoniou and van Harmelen, 2004).

## OWL

OWL, or Web Ontology Language, is used to publish and share ontologies that support advanced web searching, software agents and knowledge management. In February 2004, W3C released the RDF and the OWL as W3C recommendations (www.w3.org/2001/sw/). While XML and RDF facilitate the tagging and representation of data, it is important to have an ontology language that can formally describe the meaning of terminology used in web resources. OWL is such an ontology language. It is designed for use by applications that need to process the content of information in web resources. It provides vocabulary and semantics so that machines can interpret the content of web documents.

OWL provides three expressive sublanguages: OWL Lite, OWL DL and OWL Full. These have been designed for specific communities of implementers and users. The three types of OWL are defined as follows (W3C, 2004):

- OWL Lite is meant for those users who primarily need a classification hierarchy and simple constraints; it provides a quick migration path for thesauri and other taxonomies.
- OWL DL is meant for those users who want maximum expressiveness; it includes all OWL language constructs, but they can be used only under certain restrictions.
- OWL Full is meant for those users who want maximum expressiveness, and the syntactic freedom of RDF; it allows for vocabulary expansion and provides flexibility of classification.

OWL Lite uses only some features of OWL; it has more limitations on the use of these features than OWL DL or OWL Full. Ontology developers should choose an OWL sublanguage that meets their needs. For example, the choice between the OWL DL subsets DL Lite and DL Full depends on user requirements as regards expressiveness. The choice between OWL DL and OWL Full depends on the extent to which the meta-modelling facilities of RDF schema – defining classes, or attaching properties to classes, for example – are required.

The following are some OWL Lite features described on the W3C website. Note that the prefixes 'rdf:' or 'rdfs:' are used when terms are already present in RDF or RDF schema; terms introduced by OWL do not have any prefixes (W3C, 2004):

1 Class: a group of individuals who belong together because they share some properties. For example, Sudatta and Gobinda are both members of the class 'Person'. Classes can be organized in a specialization hierarchy using subClassOf.

2 rdfs:subClassOf: a class may be created as a subclass of another class, and thus it is possible to create a hierarchy. For example, the class 'Person' may be stated to be a subclass of the class 'Mammal'. From this it is possible to deduce that if an individual is a Person, then s/he is also a Mammal.

3 rdf:Property: properties can be used to describe the relationships between individuals, or between individuals and data values. For example, properties of the class Person may include hasChild, hasRelative, hasSibling and hasAge. The first three properties (hasChild, hasRelative and hasSibling) can be used to relate an instance of a class Person to another instance of the class Person, while the last property (hasAge) can be used to relate an instance of the class Person to an instance of the datatype Integer. Both owl:ObjectProperty and owl:DatatypeProperty are subclasses of the RDF class rdf:Property.

4 rdfs:subPropertyOf: a property may be the subproperty of one or more properties. Thus it is possible to create a hierarchy of properties. For example, hasSibling may be a subproperty of hasRelative. From this it can be deduced that if an individual is related to another by the hasSibling property, then s/he is also related to the other by the hasRelative property.

5 rdfs:domain: a property may be limited to a specific domain, thus limiting the individuals to which the property can be applied. If an individual is related to another individual by a property, and the property has a class as one of its domains, then the individuals must each belong to the class. For example, the property hasChild may be stated to have the domain Mammal, and from this it can be deduced that if John hasChild Liz, then John must be a Mammal.

6 rdfs:range: a property can have a limit, and this limit is denoted by a range. If a property relates one individual to another individual, and the property has a class as its range, then the other individual must belong to that class. For example, the property hasChild may be stated to have the range of Mammal, and then if Liz is related to John by the hasChild property (i.e. Liz is the child of John), then it can be deduced that Liz is a Mammal.

7 Individual: individuals are instances of classes, and one individual may be related to another by properties. For example, an individual named Gobinda may be described as an instance of the class Person, and the property hasEmployer may be used to relate the individual Gobinda to the individual Strathclyde University.

There are strict notions of compatibility between the OWL sublanguages. For example, every legal OWL Lite ontology is also a legal OWL DL ontology, and every legal OWL DL ontology is also a legal OWL Full ontology. Similarly, every valid OWL Lite conclusion is a valid OWL DL conclusion, and every OWL DL conclusion is a valid OWL Full conclusion (Antoniou and van Harmelen, 2004).

## Ontology: role in information organization and management

Thesauri and subject heading lists may be considered 'lightweight' ontologies, and have long been used in information organization and retrieval. Some examples of the use of thesauri in online databases and digital libraries appear in Chapter 6.

Ontologies can play a significant role in resolving information access problems in the digital world by providing a framework of shared and controlled vocabulary management and applications, thereby facilitating the machine processing of information based on semantics. An ontology defines a vocabulary (specifies its properties, values, restrictions, etc.) with which queries and assertions are exchanged among computer programmes like agents.

Antoniou and van Harmelen (2004) provide a number of examples of ontologies resolving information access problems in the digital world. One example they cite relates to the large publisher Elsevier. Like any other publisher, Elsevier's products are organized by subject, journal, volumes, issue, etc. Conventional organization and indexing approaches make it difficult to gather information from journals from different disciplines. For example, information on bird flu may appear in journals on medical sciences and biology to ornithology, and on pharmaceutical sciences to farming. Although keyword searches may produce some results, they are not always ideal. Elsevier is experimenting with using semantic web technologies to provide better access to information through the use of RDF (used as a format to exchange data between heterogeneous data sources) and an ontology (EMTREE, Elsevier's life science thesaurus).

Fensel (2001) provides a number of examples of the use of ontology in e-commerce and knowledge management. Several interesting examples of the application of ontology and semantic web technology in large business and government organizations and education are also provided by Antoniou and van Harmelen (2004).

## Summary

Although the term 'ontology' originated in philosophy a long time ago, it has been used in the information science literature only recently. Ontologies are special tools that have many similarities with vocabulary control tools like thesauri and taxonomies. Ontology building tools like Protégé and ontology languages like OWL are used to build domain- and application-specific ontologies. Several general and domain-specific ontologies have been built over the past few years, and are used to organize information in internet and intranet environments. They are used in content management activities, in building information architecture (discussed in Chapter 11) and in the context of the semantic web (discussed in Chapter 12).

## REVIEW QUESTIONS

**1** What is an ontology?

**2** What is the difference between a taxonomy, a thesaurus and an ontology?

**3** What is an ontology language and what are its major attributes?

**4** What is OWL?

**5** What role is played by ontology in information processing and management?

## References

Antoniou, G. and van Harmelen, F. (2004) *A Semantic Web Primer*, MIT Press.

Denny, M. (2002) Ontology Building: a survey of editing tools. On XML.com, www.xml.com/pub/a/2002/11/06/ontologies.html.

Denny, M. (2004) Ontology Tools Survey, Revisited. On XML.com, www.xml.com/pub/a/2004/07/14/onto.html.

Ding, Y. and Foo, S. (2002a) Ontology Research and Development. Part 1 – a review of ontology generation, *Journal of Information Science*, **28** (2), 123–36.

Ding, Y. and Foo, S. (2002b) Ontology Research and Development. Part 2 – a review of ontology mapping and evolving, *Journal of Information Science*, **28** (5), 375–88.

Fensel, D. (2001) *Ontologies: a silver bullet for knowledge management and electronic commerce*, Springer.

Gilchrist, A. (2003) Thesauri, Taxonomies and Ontologies: an etymological note, *Journal of Documentation*, **59** (1), 7–18.

Gilchrist, A. (2004) The Taxonomy: a mechanism, rather than a tool, that needs a strategy for development and application. In Gilchrist, A. and Mahon, B. (eds), *Information Architecture: designing information environments for purpose*, Facet Publishing, 192–8.

Gruber, T. R. (1993) A Translation Approach to Portable Ontology Specification, *Knowledge Acquisition*, **5** (2), 199–220.

Guarino, N. (1997) Understanding, Building and Using Ontologies: a commentary to 'Using explicit ontologies in KBS development' by Van Heijst, Schreiber, and Wielinga, *International Journal of Human and Computer Studies*, **46** (2/3), 293–310.

Guarino, N., Masolo, C. and Vetere, G. (1999 ) OntoSeek: content-based access to the Web, *IEEE Intelligent Systems*, **14** (3), (May/June), 70–80.

ISO 21127:2005 ISO/PRF 2112 *Information and Documentation: a reference ontology for the interchange of cultural heritage information*, International Standards Organization.

Jannink, J., Pichai, S., Verheijen, D. and Wiederhold, G. (1998) Encapsulation and compositon of ontologies. In *Proceedings of AAAI Workshop on Information Integration*, http://dbpubs.stanford.edu/pub/1998-17.

McGuinness, D. L. (2003) Ontologies Come of Age. In Fensel, D., Hendler, J., Lieberman, H. and Wahlster W. (eds), *Spinning the Semantic Web: bringing the worldwide web to its full potential*, MIT Press, 171–94.

Pidcock, W. (2003) *What are the Differences between a Vocabulary, a Taxonomy, a Thesaurus, an Ontology, and a Meta-model?* www.metamodel.com/article.php?story=20030115211223271.

Uschold, M. and Gruninger, M. (1996) Ontologies: principles, methods, and applications, *Knowledge Engineering Review*, **11** (2), 93–155.

Vickery, B. C. (1997) Ontologies, *Journal of Information Science*, **23** (4), 277–86.

Warner, A. J. (2004) Information Architecture and Vocabularies for Browse and Search. In Gilchrist, A. and Mahon, B. (eds) *Information Architecture: designing information environments for purpose*, Facet Publishing, 177–91.

W3C (2004) *OWL Web Ontology Language Guide*, www.w3.org/TR/owl-features/.

# 11
# Information architecture

## Introduction

Most organizations now produce and use a huge volume and variety of information on the internet and on their intranets. Many of these information resources have been designed and developed over the years as organizations have embraced and adapted to internet and web technologies. As a result, these resources are often not properly organized; in most cases information has been created and organized by a range of individuals, without full consideration of users and their requirements. This has caused enormous problems with finding and retrieving the correct information at the right time with the minimum effort. Fortunately the problem has been recognized, and many organizations now employ appropriate mechanisms for creating and organizing web and intranet information resources. The area of study concerned with the appropriate organization of web and intranet resources to facilitate easy access to, and management of, information is called 'information architecture' (IA). Library and information professionals are experienced in organizing information resources in accordance with user requirements, and consequently they have a great deal to contribute to the field of IA. This chapter provides an introduction to IA. First it describes what an IA is and what role it plays in the organization and processing of electronic information. It then goes on to discuss how to build an IA, detailing the stages involved, and outlines the expected outcome of an IA exercise.

## What is IA?

The term 'information architecture' (IA) was coined by Richard Saul Wurman in 1975, but was first used in information science in the context of organizing websites and intranets by Lou Rosenfeld and Peter Morville in 1996 (Barker, 2005; Rosenfeld and Morville, 2002).

The Information Architecture Institute (2005) defines IA as the art and science of organizing and labelling websites, intranets, online communities and software to support usability and findability. The basic objective of IA is to facilitate access to the web and institutional resources. An IA specifies the way information is labelled and grouped, and the navigation methods and terminology used within the system. Thus, an effective IA enables users to access required information easily, intuitively and confidently (Barker, 2005). Mahon and Gilchrist (2004) emphasize that an information architecture should be domain-specific and therefore should be considered in the context of the organization for which it is built.

IA involves a coherent set of strategies and plans for access to, and delivery of, information within organizations. In order to design an effective IA for an institution one should have an understanding of the institution's business objectives and constraints, the content and, most importantly, the requirements of the people who will use the site (Mahon, Hourican and Gilchrist, 2001).

## Why do we need an IA?

The major function of IA is to organize websites and intranets containing information resources and software so that users can easily and intuitively find and use the required information. Several driving forces behind IA have been identified (e.g. Barker, 2005). The main driving forces are:

- The need for proper access to, and sharing of, information: in the information age every action and decision made in an organization should be driven by access to, use of and sharing of appropriate information.
- Increasing volume of digital information: increasingly, the information created and used in an organization is digital.
- Uncoordinated and unplanned creation and management of information: different un-coordinated efforts as regards the creation and organization of electronic information within an organization over a period of time create chaos and difficulties in finding and using information.
- Heterogeneous information resources: most organizations now have to deal with heterogeneous information resources, each with its own interface and access requirements.

- Fast growth of information: rapid growth in the volume and variety of information resources is creating information overload and calling for more efficient methods of information management.
- Difficulties related to query formulation: users are not always able to formulate and conduct effective searches to meet their specific information needs.
- Different, and often non-standard, use of vocabulary: a variety of (often local and non-standard) vocabularies and jargons are used to label information resources and systems.

In addition, there are external factors that force us to take measures directed towards improving the handling and management of information within an organization. Such external factors include, for example, the Freedom of Information Act, which forces organizations not only to use information to back up every action, but also to preserve it for future reference by anyone within or outside the organization. IA provides a way to organize information resources in a given domain in order to facilitate efficient management, access and use.

## What does IA involve?

Although IA is a relatively new area of study, it has drawn tremendous attention from researchers from different fields, ranging from library and information studies to computing, the internet, government, business and industry. For example, several leading researchers and international experts are now working together at the Information Architecture Institute (formerly the Asilomar Institute for Information Architecture or AIfIA) to advance and promote the field of information architecture (Information Architecture Institute, 2005). Peter Morville, an IA pioneer, argues that IA involves traditional library and information science (LIS) skills in the design of websites and intranets, supplemented by skills in the related fields of user studies and usability engineering (Morville, 2004). Supporting the views of Morville and associates at Argus Associates (http://argus-acia.com/), Mahon and Gilchrist (2004) suggest that the LIS profession has all the skill sets necessary in the new field of IA. Their book *Information Architecture: designing information environments for purpose*, a pioneering work on IA from the perspective of library and information professionals, describes how LIS skills can fit with other technical skills to meet the overall objectives of IA. They also argue that the traditional roles of records managers, archivists and library and information professionals are converging in the new domain of IA.

## How does one build an IA?

An IA promises better organization of information resources on heterogeneous platforms so that users can find information easily and intuitively. Arms, Blanchi and Overly (1997) comment that an IA should follow basic principles such as:

■ Users and their application programmes must be given flexibility.
■ Collections must be straightforward to manage.
■ An IA must reflect the economic, social and legal frameworks within its users' work.

Thus, in order to build an effective IA, one should have a clear understanding of:

1 The components of an information model: good information models help organizations deal with information overload and facilitate the effective and efficient selection, management and use of information of different kinds – both structured, such as in databases, and unstructured, such as in documents. 'An information model is created as a set of documented information structures, information processes, standards and guidelines for implementation' (Fisher, 2004, 7).
2 The hardware and software environment: different users within an organization often work in different hardware and software environments. Since the role of an effective IA is to facilitate the finding of, access to and use of information, its design should be guided by a clear understanding, including compatibility considerations, of the hardware, software and network environments, with special reference to:
   ◆ basic operating systems and industry standard applications software
   ◆ software for content creation and management
   ◆ software and tools for information access and use, including information retrieval software and user interfaces: Wiggins (2004) and Gregory (2004) provide a set of useful guidelines for the selection and procurement of software for IA.

**3** Tools for creating and managing content: a variety of people and stakeholders may be responsible for creating different types of content within an organization. Also, a significant amount of information from outside the organization will be accessed and used for a variety of reasons. Standard software will facilitate easy access to, and exchange of, information. One of the most important roles of an IA is to annotate every item of information using appropriate and standard metadata so as to faciliate the identification, management of and access to information resources.

**4** The terminology: a major information management problem is created when non-standard terminology is used to denote various information resources and their components. One of the most important roles of an IA is to enable people to use a standard vocabulary for all items, actions, etc.

## Building an IA: approaches and stages

Several case studies reported in the IA book edited by Gilchrist and Mahon (2004), and several journal and conference papers, most notably from the ASIST (American Society for Information Science and Technology) IA research summits (www.iasummit.org/2007/), provide interesting guidelines and outline the practical experience of those who have built IAs in different industry sectors. There are basically two main approaches to building an information architecture (Barker, 2005):

- the top-down approach, where one needs to develop first a broad understanding of business strategies and user needs to define the high level structure of the site, and then a detailed understanding of the relationships between content and user needs
- the bottom-up approach, which involves an understanding of the detailed relationships between content and user requirements, which facilitates the creation of a higher level structure to support those user requirements.

Barker (2005) contends that both these techniques are important in an IA project; he also cautions that a project that ignores top-down approaches may result in well organized, findable content that does not meet user or business requirements. On the other hand, a project that ignores bottom-up approaches may result in a system that allows people to find information but does not provide them the opportunity to explore all the potentially relevant content.

Describing the development of an IA project at the UK Department of Trade and Industry, Maclachlan (2004) reports that a working group formed for the purpose focused on three main points and identified their basic requirements:

**1** Structure: the structure of the IA should be reliable and follow appropriate standards in relation to metadata and taxonomy.

**2** Navigation: the navigation should be simple and easy to use. On a technical level it should be concerned with using standard search engines and a controlled vocabulary; on a management level it should take appropriate measures for data access control, security, privacy, etc.

**3** Content: the system should be able to deal with information created by and acquired from other sources, and should also be able to deal with information created within the organization. Appropriate metadata, and an appropriate taxonomy and thesaurus, should be developed/used.

Barker (2005) suggests the following nine stages for creating an effective information architecture:

**1** Understand the nature of the organization, its business requirements and the various types of content (information resources) to be managed. To reach this understanding, one has to read various existing documentation and speak to various stakeholders in order to understand the business processes, information resources and people involved.

**2** Conduct card sorting exercises with representative users and evaluate the output. Card sorting is an exercise that allows users to classify information items in their own way; it provides a very useful insight into classification requirements.

**3** Develop a draft (paper-based) information architecture consisting of information groupings and hierarchy.

**4** Evaluate the draft information architecture using the card-based classification evaluation technique. This is the first draft and the final version may be produced after several iterations.

**5** Document the information architecture in a site map. This will be the first draft.

**6** Define a number of common user tasks and prepare page layouts to illustrate how the user will go through the site in order to accomplish those tasks. This technique is known as storyboarding.

**7** Let the members of the project team walk through the storyboards, and ask for their comments.

**8** Conduct a task-based usability test on paper prototypes and modify the design accordingly.

**9** Create detailed page layouts, along with appropriate guidance for visual designers and developers, to support the key user tasks.

## Outcome of an IA exercise

An information architecture project may go through several stages and produce several types of output. Some of the most common ones are (Barker, 2005; Doss, 2002):

**1** Site maps: these are high level diagrams showing the information structure of an organization. They can be used as the first step in laying out the information architecture of a site, and provide the framework for site navigation. They are the most widely known and understood deliverables from the process of defining an IA.

**2** Page layouts: variously termed wireframes, blue prints or screen details, page layouts define page level navigation, content types and functional elements. They are useful for conveying the general page structure and content requirements of individual pages on the site. Sometimes annotations are added to page layouts, in order to provide guidance for designers using the page layouts to build the site.

**3** Page templates: these are used when building large-scale websites and intranets. They define the layout of common page elements, such as global navigation, content and local navigation.

**4** Personas: hypothetical archetypes, or 'stand-ins' for actual users that drive the decision-making for interface design projects (Head, 2003), personas are developed as a way of defining the archetypal users of a system. Personas are created from interviews with real and potential users, using demographic data such as age, education and job title, and, more importantly, information seeking and information use behaviour.

5 Storyboards: these are sketches showing how a user would interact with a system to complete a common task. They usually combine information from process flows, site maps, etc., and comprise screen shots or some type of graphical representation of the screens, often combined with a narrative description. Thus, they help members of the project team understand the proposed IA before the system is built.

6 Prototypes: these are designed to elicit user feedback and identify any problems quickly. Prototypes can range from a few hand-sketched designs or an electronic presentation to a detailed usability testing involving users. Prototypes are often developed to enable users and other members of the project team to comment on the architecture before the full system is built.

## Summary

IA enable us to manage electronic information more efficiently. An IA is built to manage the information resources produced and used by people within an organization, and therefore an IA designed for one business may not be entirely appropriate for another business. However, some of the tools and techniques – such as the metadata, taxonomy, thesaurus, navigation and search facilities – may be applicable to other businesses dealing with similar information resources and users, with or without some modifications.

This chapter provides a brief introduction to the concept of IA. For the interested reader there are several excellent resources that discuss IA from the perspective of the information professional. Gilchrist and Mahon's book (2004) presents several case studies and examples of IA built for different types of business and institution. The Information Architecture Institute (2005) provides very useful resources on IA, and the Argus Center for Information Architecture (http://argus-acia.com/) provides a set of useful resources and a bibliography of literature on IA.

## REVIEW QUESTIONS

1 What is IA?
2 What are the goals of an IA exercise?
3 What are the major driving forces behind IA?

**4** How can LIS skills be beneficial in building an IA?
**5** What are the various outcomes of an IA exercise?

## References

Arms, W. Y., Blanchi, C. and Overly, E. A. (1997) An Architecture for Information in Digital Libraries, *D-Lib Magazine*, **3**, (February) www.dlib.org/dlib/february97/cnri/02arms1.html#info-arch.

Barker, I. (2005) *What is Information Architecture?*, www.steptwo.com.au/papers/kmc_whatisinfoarch/.

Doss, G. (2002) *Information Architecture Deliverables*, www.gdoss.com/web_info/information_architecture_deliverables.php.

Fisher, M. (2004) Developing an Information Model for Information- and Knowledge-based Organizations. In Gilchrist, A. and Mahon, B. (eds), *Information Architecture: designing information environments for purpose*, Facet Publishing.

Gilchrist, A. and Mahon, B. (eds) (2004) *Information Architecture: designing information environments for purpose*, Facet Publishing.

Gregory, J. (2004) The Care and Feeding of Software Vendors for IA Environments. In Gilchrist, A. and Mahon, B. (eds), *Information Architecture: designing information environments for purpose*, Facet Publishing.

Head, A. J. (2003) Personas: setting the stage for building usable information sites, *Online Information*, **27** (3), www.infotoday.com/online/jul03/head.shtml.

Information Architecture Institute (2005) http://iainstitute.org/.

Maclachlan, L. (2004) From Architecture to Construction: the electronic records management programme at the DTI. In Gilchrist, A. and Mahon, B. (eds), *Information Architecture: designing information environments for purpose*, Facet Publishing.

Mahon, B. and Gilchrist, A. (2004) Introduction. In Gilchrist, A. and Mahon, B. (eds), *Information Architecture: designing information environments for purpose*, Facet Publishing.

Mahon, B., Hourican, R. and Gilchrist, A. (2001) *Research into Information Architecture: the roles of software, taxonomies and people*, TFPL.

Morville, P. (2004) A Brief History of Information Architecture. In Gilchrist, A. and Mahon, B. (eds), *Information Architecture: designing information environments for purpose*, Facet Publishing.

Rosenfeld, L. and Morville, P. (2002) *Information Architecture for the World Wide Web*, O'Reilly.

Wiggins, B. (2004) Specifying and Procuring Software. In Gilchrist, A. and Mahon, B. (eds), *Information Architecture: designing information environments for purpose*, Facet Publishing.

# 12
# The semantic web

## Introduction

Within the last decade the web has grown faster than any other technology and it has now entered and influenced virtually all areas of modern life. The volume of information available on the web is huge and growing. Creation and distribution of material on the web can be achieved by any individual or institution, ranging from the school child to the professional; from big companies to academic and research institutions, governments, and national, regional and international organizations. Easy creation of, and access to, information resources on the web has been possible due to the development and use of some simple technologies, mainly HTML and related markup language technologies and protocols like HTTP. We can access information resources anywhere on the web using web search tools. While the web has indeed made our life a lot easier in terms of the creation, distribution and use of electronic information, current web technology does not allow computers to integrate and process data semantically across the internet. Tim Berners-Lee, the originator of the web, envisages the semantic web as a web of 'machine-readable information whose meaning is well defined by standards' (Berners-Lee, 2003, ix). The semantic web is based on interoperable technologies and infrastructure that will allow computers to integrate and process information according to its meaning and intended use. This chapter provides an introduction to the concept of the semantic web. It begins with a discussion of the basic concept of semantic web and how it differs from the conventional web. It then summarizes the basic semantic web technologies, particularly RDF and OWL; and, finally, discusses these with special reference to the processing of, and access to, electronic information based on semantics or meaning.

## What is the semantic web?

This is a controversial issue; some say that the semantic web is still a concept we are far from making a reality, while others, including W3C, claim that we have already developed a number of tools and appropriate technologies that can be used to realize at least some of its goals. This chapter and Chapter 13 outline the latest developments in technology and its applications that are leading towards semantic information access and management.

The following two quotations provide a basic definition and explain the main objectives of the semantic web:

> The Semantic Web is an extension of the current web in which information is given well-defined meaning, better enabling computers and people to work in cooperation.                          (Berners-Lee, Hendler and Lassila, 2001)

> The Semantic Web provides a common framework that allows data to be shared and reused across application, enterprise, and community boundaries. It is a collaborative effort led by W3C with participation from a large number of researchers and industrial partners. It is based on the Resource Description Framework (RDF), which integrates a variety of applications using XML for syntax and URIs for naming.                          (W3C, 2006)

These statements indicate that the objective of the semantic web is to use appropriate technologies so that computers can access, share and process data from various applications. Berners-Lee (1998) argues that, as opposed to the artificial intelligence approach that aims to train and use machines that can act like human beings, the objective of the semantic web is to develop languages that human beings can use for expressing information that can be processed by machines. Palmer (2001) provides a much simpler definition of the semantic web:

> The semantic web is a mesh of information linked up in such a way as to be easily processable by machines, on a global scale. You can think of it as being an efficient way of representing data on the World Wide Web, or as globally linked databases.

So the basic idea behind the semantic web is rather simple but unique: it does not aim to produce intelligent machines or intelligent software tools to understand, retrieve and link information based on their semantics. It aims to build technologies, standards and tools that would enable human beings to create information resources on the web in such a way that specially designed computer programs can read and process the information from those documents easily and on a global scale.

## How does the semantic web differ from the conventional web?

As opposed to current web technologies, which are designed to facilitate human access to information from a variety of web resources, semantic web technology is primarily designed for computers. Its target is to access, share and process data – as opposed to information resources or documents.

Currently we use web search tools to access information resources; although it is very easy to search for and retrieve a large number of documents using these search tools, a closer look at current web technologies will reveal a number of problems. For example:

1 Information access is based primarily on keyword searches. Although information retrieval techniques can be used to define different variations of search terms, location and proximity of search terms, frequency of search terms, etc., the retrieval is still based on word matching rather than on meaning and semantics.
2 In most cases web search engines produce a large number of hits, and it is practically impossible to check all the retrieved items manually to determine their relevance to the query. Even though the search results are often ranked, the top-ranking documents are not necessarily the most relevant to the query.
3 The results of a web search are web pages possibly containing the required information; a search does not always produce a specific answer to a question, except in a few specialized web search tools. Pages are retrieved based on the occurrence within them of the search terms, and the user is expected to read them and decide on their suitability.
4 Results do not integrate data from different pages and/or sites. Some specific applications, such as web-based flight or hotel information systems, search and gather data from several sites, but they are proprietary systems: it is not possible for general agents (in the context of the internet, an agent is a specially designed programme

that gathers information or performs specific tasks on a regular schedule) to access and use the data in proprietary databases.

**5** Much of the data available on the web are not sharable and reusable among various applications.

The semantic web promises to overcome these problems with technologies that will facilitate data access, processing, sharing and reuse by computers. It will not involve building intelligent agents or systems on top of the current web; instead simple technologies will be used to create web data which can be then accessed and processed by computer based on meaning, intended use, imposed restrictions, etc.

So, will the semantic web improve information retrieval on the web? In the words of Tim Berners-Lee, the semantic web is not for finding things more easily: it is about 'creating things from data you've compiled yourself, or combining it with volumes (think databases, not so much individual documents) of data from other sources to make new discoveries. It's about the ability to use and reuse vast volumes of data' (Updegrove, 2005). He further emphasizes that the semantic web is not meant to facilitate better access to documents; rather, it is designed to interconnect personal information management, enterprise application integration and the global sharing of commercial, scientific and cultural data. Access to and sharing of data is the primary focus of the semantic web: its emerging technologies facilitate access to information based on semantics, thereby paving the way for semantic information retrieval that is not based on artificial intelligence or knowledge-based techniques, but on machine-processable data.

## Semantic web technologies

Tim Berners-Lee proposed a layered approach to the semantic web, with the idea that once the standards, tools, etc., are built for one layer, and are agreed on by the stakeholders, work may begin on the next layer (Berners-Lee, 2003). Two basic principles are followed in this approach (Antoniou and Harmelen, 2004):

■ downward compatibility: agents fully aware of one layer should be able to take full advantage of – i.e., interpret and use – information written at lower levels

- upward compatibility: agents fully aware of one layer should take at least partial advantage of information at higher levels.

At the bottom layer there is XML, which allows the writing of structured web documents, using user-defined vocabulary. There are also XML schemas, which control the structure of XML documents. These technologies basically allow the user to create and send web documents across the web.

At the next layer are the RDF and RDF schemas. RDF is the data model for writing simple statements about web resources, whereas an RDF schema provides a model for organizing web objects into hierarchies by assigning properties, subproperty and subclass relationships, and domain and range restrictions.

Next there is the ontology layer, and on top of that there is the logic layer, which is used to enhance the ontology layer further for the writing of applications. The two final layers, proof then trust, ensure proof validation and trust through the use of cryptography and digital signatures (used for encoding and ensuring authenticity of data) as required.

The semantic web is based on the following technologies (Balani, 2005; Palmer, 2001; W3C, 2006):

- URI (uniform resource identifier), a global naming scheme
- RDF (resource description framework), a standard syntax for describing data
- RDF schema, a standard means for describing the properties of that data
- ontologies, a standard means for describing relationships between data items, defined by OWL (Web Ontology Language).

## URI

A URI, or a uniform resource identifier, as the name suggests, is a specific code or identification assigned to a web resource that uniquely identifies it. It consists of a string of characters denoting a name or an address that can be used to refer to a resource. The string has to conform to a certain generic syntax (Berners-Lee, 2001).

So, how does a URI differ from a URL or a URN? A URL, or a uniform resource locator, is a locator (or, simply speaking an address) for a network accessible resource (Peacock, 1998). On the other hand, a URI identifies a resource and tells us how to access the resource by specifying its location. For example, www.strath.ac.uk is a URI that identifies the resource as the website of Strathclyde University, and also tells us that the website can be accessed at a particular address via HTTP. Thus, while a URL identifies the location or container for an instance of a resource, a URI identifies a resource that may reside in one or more locations, may move, or may not be available at a given time. A URN, or uniform resource name, is a URI that identifies a resource by a name. As opposed to a URL, it only denotes the name of the resource; it does not say how to locate or obtain it.

Every data object and every data model on the semantic web must have a unique URI that identifies a resource by name in a particular namespace. Tim Berners-Lee (1998) developed a general specification for URI (RFC2717), and, although a general URI naming scheme was produced by W3C, it was subsequently abandoned because it became too unwieldy to maintain (www.w3.org/addressing/schemes). The Internet Standard List of URI Schemes is maintained by IANA (Internet Assigned Numbers Authority), which co-ordinates various standard naming services on the internet such as domain name services, IP address services, etc. (www.iana.org/).

## RDF

The RDF is a framework for describing and interchanging data on the web. It is a specification that defines a model for representing the world, and a syntax for structuring, representing and exchanging that model (Balani, 2005). It provides a consistent, standardized way in which to describe and query all kinds of web resources, ranging from texts and images to audio files and video clips.

The fundamental concepts within RDF are resources, properties and statements (Antoniou and van Harmelen, 2004). A resource in the context of RDF is an object that we deal with. Resources can be people, products, books, hotels – anything. Every resource has a URI or uniform resource identifier (Peacock, 1998). Properties describe relations between resources. Examples of properties are: 'written by' in the case of a book as a resource, 'age' in the case of a person as a resource and 'price' in the case of a product as a resource. Properties can have their own properties; they can be found and manipulated like any other resource. A statement in RDF is described as a triplet consisting of a resource, a property and a value.

RDF has a number of characteristics that provide it with great flexibility:

- Independence: an individual or organization can independently invent a property – for example, the same property may be used as author by someone, and director (as in the case of a movie) by another.
- Interchange: since RDF statements can be converted into XML, they can easily be interchanged.
- Scalability: the three–part RDF statements are easy to handle and make it simple to look for and identify a resource; and they can be easily scaled up to match requirements in the web environment.

RDF allows us to define metadata about web resources, such as the title, author, date of modification, copyright and licensing information and terms of availability of a web resource (W3C, 2004b). Such metadata play a key role in providing access to web resources. RDF offers syntactic interoperability, and provides the base layer for building the semantic web.

In order for its statements to be machine-processable, RDF uses a specific XML markup language, referred to as RDF/XML, to represent RDF information and exchange it between machines (W3C, 2004b). RDF uses URI – or, more precisely, URI references or .URIref, which is a URI together with an optional fragment identifier at the end. Taking a simple example from the W3C's *RDF Primer* (2004b), the URI reference www.example.org/index.html#section2 consists of the URI www.example.org/index.html and (separated by the "#" character) the fragment identifier Section2.

So, how is RDF/XML different from HTML? RDF/XML is machine-processable, and through URIs it can link pieces of information across the web. In this respect RDF/XML performs the same function as HTML. However, unlike conventional hypertext, RDF URIs can refer to any identifiable thing, including things that may not be directly retrievable on the web – with the result that in addition to describing such things as web pages, RDF can also describe other things such as cars, businesses, people, news events, etc. (W3C, 2004b).

A simple RDF statement consists of a subject, a predicate and an object; that is, an object has an attribute with a value. The following is a simple example of an RDF statement taken from the *RDF Primer* (W3C, 2004b).

The simple English statement: 'www.example.org/index.html has a creator whose value is John Smith' can be represented in an RDF statement having:

- a subject, www.example.org/index.html
- a predicate, http://purl.org/dc/elements/1.1/creator, and
- an object, www.example.org/staffid/85740.

URIrefs are used here to identify the subject, the predicate and the object, instead of using the words 'creator' and 'John Smith'. RDF models statements as nodes and arcs in a graph. As shown in Figure 12.1, a statement is represented by a node for the subject, a node for the object and an arc for the predicate, directed from the subject node to the object node.

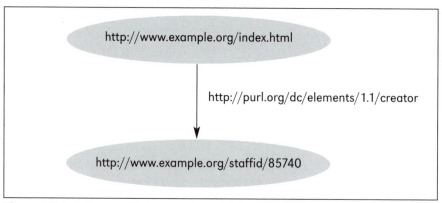

**Figure 12.1** A simple RDF statement (www.w3.org/TR/rdf-primer/#conceptsummary)

Objects in RDF statements may be either .URIrefs or literals with constant values represented by character strings, in order to represent certain kinds of property values. In RDF graphs, nodes that are URIrefs are shown as ellipses, while nodes that are literals are shown as boxes. Figure 12.2 shows some literal values as well as .URIrefs.

RDF is a data model that allows us to present data in XML, but essentially it is domain-independent and no assumptions are made about domain. However, users can define their own terminology in using an RDF schema or RDFS. It should be noted that RDF schemas and XML schemas are not similar; XML schemas constrain the structure of XML

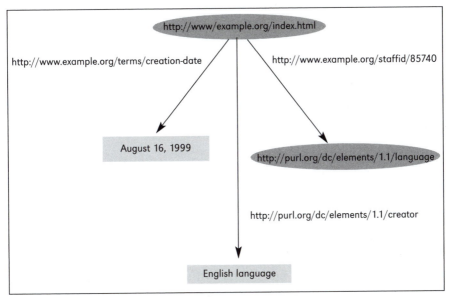

**Figure 12.2** Several statements about the same resource
(www.w3.org/TR/rdf-primer/#conceptsummary)

documents, while RDF schemas define the vocabulary used in RDF data models (Antoniou and van Harmelen, 2004).

RDF provides a model for metadata, and a syntax so that computers can exchange it and use it. However, it does not provide any properties of its own. For example, it doesn't define author, title or business category, etc., or the relationships among various objects and properties in a given domain. This is done by the domain-specific RDF schema. However, an RDF schema is limited to the subclass hierarchy and subproperty hierarchy within the limits of the relevant property domain and range definitions (W3C, 2004b). Ontology languages, like DAML+OIL and OWL, are required for writing explicit and formal conceptualizations of domain models. Although RDF and RDFS allow us to represent a significant amount of semantic information in terms of subclass and subproperty hierarchies, they are restrictive in the following ways (Antoniou and van Harmelen, 2004):

- Although we can define the range of a property, we cannot declare that the range applies to some classes only, for example that some people are vegetarians while others are not.
- In an RDF schema we can state a subclass, but we can't show that

two subclasses with the same superclass are disjoint, for example male and female are disjoint classes but both are a subclass of person.

■ RDF schema do not permit the Boolean combination of disjoint classes to define a class.

■ Special restrictions such as one, many, mandatory or optional – for example a course is taught by at least one lecturer, or a student must have one and only one registration number – cannot be expressed in RDF schema.

■ An RDF schema does not permit the formulation of special characteristics, so we cannot define a property as transitive, unique or the inverse of another property.

## Semantic web applications

Current web technology enables us primarily to search for and access information within documents. Although several web applications have been built that use data files in the form of databases, spreadsheets, etc. – for example airline or hotel booking systems, or the book ordering system on Amazon – all these applications use data created and/or organized for a specific application. In fact, current web technology does not provide a mechanism for publishing data in such a way that it can be easily processed by anyone. Although a huge volume and variety of data are now available – for example, airline and railway timetables, weather information, population and census data, etc. – it is currently not possible to use this data in particularly flexible ways. Semantic web aims to resolve this problem. The semantic web technologies will enable people and organizations to publish data in a reusable and repurposable form

Thus, the semantic web will integrate large amounts of data from a range of applications, and process them on the fly in order to produce meaningful outcomes. Tim Berners-Lee suggests that examples of such applications may include, say, 'financial models for oil futures, discovering the synergies between biology and chemistry researchers in the Life Sciences, or getting the best price and service on a new pair of hiking boots' (Updegrove, 2005).

Semantic web technology may bring significant developments in application areas like knowledge management, e-commerce and agent technologies, and thus may provide better knowledge management facilities in a number of ways. For example (Antoniou and Harmelen, 2004):

- Knowledge could be organized according to its meaning.
- Automated tools could be built to check for inconsistencies and to extract new and useful knowledge.
- Question-answering may replace conventional keyword searching, and requested information may be presented in a more meaningful way.
- Knowledge could be extracted from several resources and sites, and similarly could be shared among several computers and sites.
- Access to specific knowledge may be managed more easily, playing a role in deciding who can have access to what information.

Similarly, the semantic web can facilitate e-commerce in a number of ways. For example:

- Software agents and tools could be built to extract pricing and product information easily.
- Privacy and security issues may be managed more efficiently.
- Tools could be built to compare and evaluate companies and products more efficiently for consumers.
- More sophisticated agents could be developed to produce lists of the best offers or the best choices available, based on consumer requirements and the products available in the market.
- Better partnerships and collaborations will be fostered by improved automatic knowledge processing, interchange and sharing across various applications.

The semantic web could play a significant role in facilitating personal use of the web. Antoniou and Harmelen (2004) provide an interesting example of how the semantic web could facilitate the working of a personal agent in proposing a solution by capturing and processing data from various applications. In essence, by providing technology for machines to share machine-processable data across various applications, the semantic web could significantly improve the use of the web.

## Semantic web and information access

As discussed earlier in this chapter, the primary objectives of the semantic web are to facilitate access to information and to process and share machine-processable data on the web. Thus the semantic web will facilitate information processing and management by creating an environment for access, sharing, processing and reusing distributed data across various platforms and organizations. But will the semantic web have any impact on information access and retrieval?

Libraries and information systems have over the years developed tools, techniques and standards for providing access to information from a variety of sources and channels. So, will the semantic web improve the information access and management activities performed by library and information systems? In order to answer this question we need to take a quick look at the current issues and problems facing library and information systems with regard to access and the management of heterogeneous information.

Libraries and the other so-called 'memory institutions' (Dempsey, 1999) such as archives and museums have always dealt with authoritative, high quality information created and made available by reputable and authentic sources. Traditionally, different memory organizations have managed their information resources separately using their own tools, techniques and standards. The descriptions of the information resources held within different memory organizations vary with a number of factors, such as:

- the nature, type and subject of the collections
- specific organizational approaches to organizing and processing information
- the granularity (the various components) and the level of description required to facilitate access to the resources
- the data structure and content of the metadata
- users and local needs.

These variations have forced the creation of separate standards and approaches to organizing information, and often a number of localized approaches and tools/standards have been developed to meet the specific needs of the collections, the organizations involved and the users. The web has made it possible to integrate the collections of various memory organizations, thereby making it possible to provide seamless access to their various collections and resources. However, differences in approach to information processing and management across various memory organizations seriously hinder the interoperability of systems, and thus access to cultural information resources on a global scale.

For academic and research libraries the web has brought tremendous opportunities, and they now acquire, organize and provide access to information from a wide variety of channels, including conventional publishers, aggregators (services providing access to information resources produced by different publishers), databases, digital libraries, institutional archives and the personal pre-print repositories of academics and researchers. Seamless, location-independent discovery of, organization of and access to relevant scholarly information calls for interoperability among resources, however and wherever they are physically hosted. This has remained a major problem in the scholarly information management world; there is a need for highly scalable, interoperable and yet simple human-independent systems for sharing, processing and using information distributed throughout the web.

Indeed, the need to support a wide variety of types and sources of metadata, to integrate them effectively and to expose them to successfully simple, flexible search and retrieval tools has become a major challenge for libraries in the web era (*MIT SIMILE Proposal*, 2005). The semantic web promises the solution: making information available on the web in a way that facilitates its effective discovery, processing, integration and reuse across various applications. Several research projects have been undertaken to use semantic web technologies to facilitate seamless access to scholarly information over the web. SIMILE is one such project, undertaken by MIT libraries and W3C, aiming to create useful tools to enhance information management capabilities at low cost and with high scalability (*MIT SIMILE Proposal*, 2005). These tools and technologies, once fully built and implemented, will enable libraries to act as data source themselves – for example, by capturing relevant data from various applications and/or by offering recommendation services based on individual or collective patterns of use and interests in digital information. Several other, similar or related, research efforts have been made in the recent past. The CIDOC Conceptual Reference Model (CIDOC CRM; Crofts et al., 2003) is a robust domain ontology for the exchange of rich cultural heritage data. It employs data modelling techniques to formalize the semantic concepts used in memory organizations – libraries, archives and museums – in order to facilitate data exchange (Gill, 2004).

Semantic web technologies will have a significant impact on information retrieval, especially in semantic retrieval and automatic question–answer systems. Ontology languages like OWL, which support logic inferences, can facilitate more flexible and precise knowledge representation and retrieval (W3C, 2004a). Shah, Finin and Joshi (2002) propose a prototype framework in which both documents and queries can be marked up with statements in the DAML+OIL semantic web language, thereby providing both structured and semi-structured information about documents and their contents, which will facilitate inferencing when a document is indexed, a query is processed or query results are evaluated.

## Summary

The web has brought about tremendous changes in the information world. The concept of the semantic web proposes yet another revolution by making it possible to access, share and reuse data and information available on the web. The key idea behind the semantic web is to facilitate the machine processing of data. Appropriate tools and techniques have been developed by various agencies under the auspices of the W3C.

Although the primary aim of the semantic web, according to its originator Berners-Lee, is to process, share and reuse data and information, as opposed to documents, semantic web technologies could be used to improve the processing and managing of information, as in documents, based on semantics or meaning. The next few years will no doubt be exciting for the information world.

## REVIEW QUESTIONS

**1** What is the semantic web?
**2** How does the semantic web differ from the conventional web?
**3** Does the semantic web mean semantic IR?
**4** What is RDF and what does it do for the semantic web?
**5** What role is played by XML in the context of the semantic web?

## References

Antoniou, G. and van Harmelen, F. (2004) *A Semantic Web Primer*, MIT Press.

Balani, N. (2005) *The Future of the Web is Semantic: ontologies form the backbone of a whole new way to understand online data*,
www-128.ibm.com/developerworks/xml/library/wa-semweb/.

Berners-Lee, T. (1998) *Semantic Web Roadmap*,
www.w3.org/designissues/semantic.html.

Berners-Lee, T. (2001) *Uniform Resource Identifiers (URI): generic syntax*,
www.ietf.org/rfc/rfc2396.txt.

Berners-Lee, T. (2003) Foreword. In Fensel, D., Hendler, J., Lieberman, H. and Wahlster, W. (eds), *Spinning the Semantic Web: bringing the worldwide web to its full potential*, MIT Press.

Berners-Lee, T., Hendler, J. and Lassila, O. (2001) The Semantic Web, *Scientific American*, **284** (5), 34–43.

Crofts, N., Doerr, M., Gill, T., Stead, S. and Stiff, M (eds) (2003) *Definition of the CIDOC Conceptual Reference Model*,
http://cidoc.ics.forth.gr/definition_cidoc.html.

Dempsey, L. (1999) A Research Framework for Digital Libraries, Museums and Archives: scientific, industrial and cultural heritage: a shared approach, *Ariadne*, www.ariadne.ac.uk/issue22/dempsey/.

Gill, T. (2004) Building Semantic Bridges between Museums, Libraries and Archives: the CIDOC conceptual reference model, *First Monday*, **9** (5), www.firstmonday.org/issues/issue9_5/gill/.

*MIT SIMILE Proposal* (2005) http://simile.mit.edu/funding/mellon_2005.pdf.

Palmer, S. B. (2001) *The Semantic Web: an introduction*,
http://infomesh.net/2001/swintro.

Peacock, I. (1998) What is . . . a URI?, *Ariadne*,
www.ariadne.ac.uk/issue18/what-is/.

Shah, U., Finin, T. and Joshi, A. (2002) Information Retrieval on the Semantic Web. In *Proceedings of the Eleventh International Conference on Information and Knowledge Management*, McLean, Virginia, 4–9 November 2002, ACM Press, 461–8.

Updegrove, A. (2005) The Semantic Web: an interview with Tim Berners-Lee, *Consortium Standards Bulletin*,
www.consortiuminfo.org/bulletins/semanticweb.php.

W3C (2001) *URIs, URLs, and URNs: clarifications and recommendations 1.0*,
www.w3.org/tr/uri-clarification/.

W3C (2004a) *OWL Web Ontology Language overview*,
www.w3.org/tr/owl-features/.

W3C (2004b) *RDF Primer*, www.w3.org/tr/2004/rec-rdf-primer-20040210/.

W3C (2006) *Semantic Web Activity*, www.w3.org/2001/sw/.

# 13
# Information organization: issues and trends

## Introduction

Organizing information has always been a complex task, and a range of tools, techniques and standards, from catalogue codes, classification schemes and subject heading lists to bibliographic formats, had to be developed to meet these challenges. These have long been used successfully in the library world for organizing, accessing and sharing information. However, the degree of complexity involved has increased enormously over the past decade or so, owing to the appearance and proliferation of internet and web technologies that have facilitated the creation, distribution and use of information by virtually anyone with access to the appropriate equipment. New tools, techniques and standards have been developed to organize and process digital information available on the internet and intranets. These include metadata standards, taxonomies, ontologies, XML, RDF, etc. The main objective of these initiatives is now to facilitate the organization and processing of information based on meaning, and the development of the semantic web. This chapter highlights new research in different areas of information organization; it aims to focus on major issues and trends. The chapter begins with a discussion of current research on cataloguing and the FRBR (Function and Requirements for Bibliographic Records) model. It then considers metadata issues, especially in the context of metadata management. The latest research related to classification, ontology and semantic portals, especially in the context of digital libraries, is then outlined. The chapter ends with a brief discussion of trends relating to recently developed approaches to user-driven information organization and processing, and thus poses some pertinent questions about the future of information organization in the digital age.

## Cataloguing: FRBR and semantic catalogue networks

While the cataloguing of scholarly publications is usually performed centrally by national libraries or agencies such as OCLC, to ensure standardization, the cataloguing of internet resources, local digital library collections and freely accessible scholarly information resources – such as those available on open archives – is not controlled by any particular agency, and this poses challenges for information professionals. Mitchell and Surratt (2005) point out that appropriate measures for cataloguing discipline-based repositories, institutional repositories and open access resources are necessary in order to record, preserve and provide access to the intellectual resources of institutional and individual scholars.

Catalogue codes have long been used in the library world to create and interlink catalogues of bibliographic records. However, the data structures used in catalogue codes were not designed to display the semantic relationships among various records in a given subject. The FRBR architecture was designed to map and display inter- and intradocument relations, and researchers believe that this will help the development of new catalogue structures capable of building a semantic network of catalogue records, as exemplified by a number of implementations reported at the 2004 annual conference of the CILIP Cataloguing and Indexing Group (CIG; see Le Boeuf, 2004a, 2005; Stillone, 2004).

Such new and promising applications of the FRBR model can be observed at the AustLit gateway (www.austlit.edu.au/), Virtua (an integrated library system from VTLS that uses FRBR, www.vtls.com/), FictionFinder (OCLC's FRBR project, www.oclc.org/research/projects/frbr/fictionfinder.htm), RedLightGreen (http://redlightgreen.com/ucwprod/web/workspace.jsp) and the FRBR Display tool (www.loc.gov/marc/marc-functional-analysis/tool.html) of the Library of Congress.

The AustLit gateway (www.austlit.edu.au/) uses the FRBR model to generate a catalogue of linked resources in Australian literature (Kilner, 2004). Le Boeuf (2004b) reports on a study that shows how the FRBR model can be used to link various musical works, fragments of musical works, and works of vocal music. He suggests that FRBR can also be used as the basis for a model to represent the complex processes involved in the production and reception of musical works. The FRBR model can also be used to organize various other non–bibliographic information resources. For example, Nicolas (2004) reports that the FRBR model allows a better treatment of oral tradition works.

Miller and Le Boeuf (2004) comment that AACR2 does not make provision for resources on live performances and, as a result, specialized institutions have developed their own rules for the description of live performances; for example, the Dance Heritage Coalition (New York) creates authority records for choreographic works, and the Département des Arts du Spectacle at the Bibliothèque Nationale de France creates bibliographic records for theatrical, operatic and choreographic performances. However, considering that the FRBR model can be used to describe live performances, an FRBR-based model for recording and handling performing arts as bibliographic entities has been proposed by Miller and Le Boeuf (2004) and Le Boeuf (2004b). Tillett (2005) suggests that the FRBR model can form the foundation for the future of cataloguing, and thus can play a key role in the development of a new edition of AACR (see Chapter 3, page 42).

However, some researchers have expressed concerns and reservations about the FRBR model and approach. For example, Beall (2006) warns:

> The unwarranted enthusiasm for the model, its complexity and ambiguity, its irrelevance to most libraries, its lack of proven success, and the potential negative impact it will have on the crosswalking of library metadata are all good reasons for taking a second look at FRBR and re-evaluating whether it should be adopted so unquestioningly.

Patrick Le Boeuf, Chair of the IFLA FRBR Review Group, believes that although revolutionary in its innovative features, the FRBR model has some elements of conservatism in its approach, which it has inherited perhaps from the logical flaws in cataloguing, and thus alternatives to FRBR may be necessary for future evolution in cataloguing (Le Boeuf, 2004a).

## Metadata

There is no centralized control over the quality or content of either the information or the embedded metadata on the web, and this adds to the complexity of the job of information creators and publishers, information access providers like search engines and, most importantly, users. The Dublin Core metadata standard was developed with the main objective of keeping metadata elements simple so that authors could create their own metadata for the resources they create. Even though tools such as

DCDOT (www.ukoln.ac.uk/metadata/dcdot/) have been built that can facilitate the automatic creation of Dublin Core metadata for web resources, the job of assigning metadata to web resources is still largely done manually by indexers. One possible alternative could be to use author-generated metadata. However, when authors create metadata, the result is not always very impressive. A recent study by Zhang and Jastram (2006) shows that often authors include too many keywords in their web pages in the hope that it will make their pages more visible, although such an approach does not always help the search engines. This study also notes that often the authors of web pages choose a handful of metadata elements that they think will make their pages more visible; the three most popular are the keyword, description and author elements while the least popular are the date, publisher and resource type elements. However, choosing these metadata fields does not always improve the chances of retrieval. Zhang and Jastram (2006) conclude that while it is widely known that metadata have the potential to improve information organization and retrieval on the internet, it is a mystery whether the internet publishing community uses metadata correctly.

The fact that metadata promise better information organization, discovery, management and access is known to IT and information (science as well as systems) people, but how to convince business managers to invest in metadata is a major question. In discussing why business managers should care about metadata, Shankaranarayanan and Even (2006) note that metadata are likely to be useful in rational, data-driven, analytical decision-making scenarios in a business environment. However, they also mention that it is not clear whether metadata provide similar benefits when the decisions to be made are more intuitive and political.

Haynes (2004) comments that, in future, users will be less aware of metadata, although some communities will have more to do with it. In order for metadata to work successfully behind the scenes, system developers will have to think specifically in terms of managing metadata, controlling their format and ensuring their interoperability across various systems and applications. On a positive note, Haynes (2004) observes that an increasing number of library and information science courses now offer modules on metadata as part of their syllabus, and as this trend continues a new inter-disciplinary subject may emerge which will in turn facilitate the convergence of practice and interests among the various sectors that work on, and are interested in, metadata.

## Classification in the digital age

The challenges of classification in the digital age are manifold. Classification systems can no longer be a 'marking and parking' device; they need to play a much wider role in access and retrieval as well as in the sharing and exchange of meaning-based information among various systems and services. Mai (2003) comments that future requirements for the international exchange of bibliographic records and interoperability among various information systems and services can be met only if general classification systems are used in conjunction with special domain-specific classification and indexing systems. Thus, general classification systems should be regarded as tools for the broad organization of knowledge, while special systems will be concerned with the domain-specific organization and representation of documents.

The most widely used examples of tools for organizing web resources using the principles of classification are the web directories, such as the Yahoo! directory. Pointing to a recent survey by the Delphi Research Group (www.delphigroup.com/) that shows that 70% of users' search time was spent browsing, and that 75% of users preferred browsing to searching, Gilchrist (2006) comments that the need for taxonomies as pioneered by Yahoo! remains very important. He further comments that these taxonomies are a sort of hybrid between classification and thesauri, although they do not follow the normal practices of either classification or thesauri, and no clear guidelines for their construction are available. Justifying the importance of facet analysis techniques in information organization and the retrieval of internet information, Broughton (2006) comments that faceted classification schemes can function very well as a tool for browsing, navigating and retrieving web information resources.

So far, efforts to organize web resources using bibliographic classification schemes like DDC, UDC, LC, etc. have remained limited to small, human-processed, specialized collections of internet resources like BUBL (www.bubl.ac.uk). Such applications are human-dependent and resource-intensive. However, researchers at OCLC and elsewhere have been trying to build automatic classification techniques using bibliographic classification schemes. OCLC's classification research focuses on two main questions (OCLC, 2006a):

■ Can classification schemes like DDC or LC be adapted to classify web resources automatically?

■ What improvements to automatic classification systems are needed to get as close to human performance as possible?

OCLC has built some open-source software called SCORPION for automatically classifying text documents on the web. It can be downloaded for free by anyone for the purpose of research into automatic classification (OCLC, 2006b). Another OCLC project is called Terminology Services (OCLC, 2006c; Vizine-Goetz, 2004; Vizine-Goetz et al., 2004) and aims to make the concepts behind knowledge organization tools, and the relationships among various knowledge organization tools, available to users and computer programs in order to facilitate information access and management. During this project direct mappings (associations based on equivalent terms) and co-occurrence mappings (associations based on the co-occurrence of terms from different schemes) have been drawn up among a number of vocabulary control tools and classification schemes: DDC, the ERIC (Education Resources Information Center) thesaurus, GSA FD (genre terms for fiction), LC, LCSH, LCSHac (LC children's headings), MeSH (Medical Subject Headings) and NLMC (National Library of Medicine Classification). Selected vocabularies, such as the GSAFD vocabulary, are available for online use and for downloading using the OAI (Open Archives Initiative) protocol (OCLC, 2006c).

## Ontologies

Taxonomies and ontologies can play different roles in the organization of, and access to, electronic information resources, in building an information architecture and in building the semantic web. Researchers have designed and used ontologies in different contexts. For example, a specially built ontology in an interdisciplinary subject can show the complex relationships among various topics, which cannot be easily shown by a conventional subject headings list. Kayo (2005) has demonstrated this by developing an ontology in the interdisciplinary area of women's studies.

Managing government information is a complex job because of legislative and administrative diversity, complex administrative hierarchies and differing implementation strategies due to central, regional and local administrative structures and policies. Prokopiadou, Papatheodorou and Moschopoulos (2004) contend that ontologies and associated tools can provide for the hierarchical representation and navigation of government information. Researchers have proposed several ontologies for managing government information (e.g. Borenstein and Brooks, 2006a, 2006b).

Despite recent research and development activities, the semantic integration of ontologies in a distributed environment remains an important challenge in the organization of knowledge in the new multimedia digital library world. Often it may be necessary to integrate more than one available ontology in the same or related disciplines. Kent (2003) describes an approach to the semantic integration of ontologies as a two-step process:

- alignment, which involves sharing common terminology and semantics through a mediating ontology
- unificatio, which involves fusion of the alignment of ontologies.

## Semantic portals and ontologies

Web portals provide access to internet resources, but building and updating portals is a resource-intensive job requiring significant human intervention. Researchers believe that semantic web portals, based on semantic web technologies, have the potential to improve the quality and effectiveness of web portals. Semantic web portals differ from conventional web portals in a number of ways (Reynolds, Shabajee and Cayzer, 2004):

- Semantic portals support multidimensional searching through a rich domain ontology.
- Unlike conventional web portals, semantic web portals allow for bottom-up evolution and decentralized updates.
- Information structure is controlled by an ontology and is machine-processable.
- It is possible to have multiple aggregations and views of the same data.
- Data can be published in reusable forms for incorporation in multiple portals.

Ontologies form the backbone of semantic web portals; they are used to create a conceptual structure for a web portal based on a formal representation of controlled terminology (Lausen et al, 2005; Reynolds, Shabajee and Cayzer, 2004; Steffen and Maedche, 2001). However, appropriate ontology management facilities are required to ensure the quality and usability of semantic web portals, and this can be challenging, especially in micro- and interdisciplinary subjects.

## Semantic web technologies and digital libraries

Semantic web technologies, especially ontologies, can play a significant role in digital and hybrid libraries. A typical library today provides access to a variety of digital information resources from various channels, ranging from local digital repositories to online databases, e-journals, remote digital libraries and the web. Providing seamless access to such varied resources calls for a mechanism that permits analysis of the meaning of resources, which will facilitate computer processing of information for improved access. Sure and Studer (2005) maintain that semantic web technologies can be used in digital libraries in the context of user interface design, user profiling, personalization and user interaction.

Semantic web technologies, especially ontologies, can be used in a number of other ways too – most importantly in supporting meaning-based information organization and access to heterogeneous and multimedia information resources. A number of web resources are now available that list various ontology-related research activities. For example, Clark (n.d.) provides an excellent resource page listing ontology projects, research groups and research works that used ontologies, and the DAML ontology library (www.daml.org/ontologies/) provides a directory of 282 ontologies organized by URI, submission date, keyword, funding source, etc.

## User-driven classification of web resources

Several user-driven tagging and classification systems for organizing web resources have emerged over the past few years. These systems, often called social classifications or folksonomies, allow users to tag and classify web resources themselves. Del.icio.us (http://del.icio.us) is just such a system, and allows users to organize web pages: users can add sites to their personal collections of links, categorize those sites with the tags or keywords of their choice and share their collections with others. Thus, instead of using standardized terminology from a vocabulary control tool or an ontology, users choose their own terminologies to describe a web resource. Flickr (www.flickr.com), a photo management and sharing web application, has a similar approach and allows free-form tagging of photos. Furl (http://furl.net/about.jsp) is another such service for the creation and sharing of web resources, which allows users to add keywords and save web pages on a personal work space that can be searched and retrieved using the user-given keywords at any time.

All these systems require users to create a user account, and are available free to anyone. The idea of these socially constructed classification schemes with no input from a professional cataloguer or information architect is novel, and it will be interesting to see how far they can improve access to, and sharing of, digital information resources. Gilchrist (2006) comments that it will be interesting to collect the end user views of folksonomies like Del.icio.us and Flickr and combine them into a structure, perhaps in the form of a topic map.

## Conclusion

Organization of information in libraries has a history extending back over 2000 years. Modern classification and cataloguing tools and principles first emerged over 125 years ago, and since then these tools and techniques have evolved within the library and information world. However, within the past decade or so the task of organizing information has become much more challenging due to the advent and proliferation of the internet and digital libraries. Within this time many new technologies, tools and standards – including metadata, ontologies, XML, RDF, etc. – have been developed for organizing and managing digital information resources. Semantic web technologies and standards are now being developed to facilitate the content-based organization of digital information, in order to facilitate better and easy access.

In parallel, a decentralized and uncontrolled approach to the organization of digital information is also taking shape, where the onus is on users to choose keywords for tagging and organizing web resources. It will be interesting to see whether these uncontrolled and user-driven approaches can produce results that are comparable to, or even better than, controlled semantic web approaches to organizing digital information.

Several developments are taking place in the construction of special digital libraries. Examples of such developments are abundant and range from specialized institutional repositories and co-operative ventures like the OAI (Open Archives Initiative) to various digital collections developed at the national and community levels, giving rise to what can be called the distributed community digital library (Chowdhury, Poulter and McMenemy, 2006). A range of innovative tools, techniques and standards will be required for the organization and management of such digital libraries and information services. Another recent development that calls for special measures for information organization is the creation of new and integrated technologies combining digital libraries, intranets, the web and VLEs (virtual learning environments) in order to create environments for technology-enhanced learning.

All these developments are bringing new challenges to LIS professionals and require them to be better prepared for, and equipped with, the appropriate tools, techniques and standards for organizing information. The job of LIS professionals remains exciting!

## References

Beall, J. (2006) Some Reservations about FRBR, *Library Hi Tech News*, **23** (2), 15–16.

Borenstein, J. and Brooks, R. (2006a) Ontology Management for Federal Agencies, *DM Review*, www.dmreview.com/article_sub.cfm?articleid=1030240.

Borenstein, J. and Brooks, R. (2006b) Ontology Management for Federal Agencies. Part 2, *DM Review*, www.dmreview.com/article_sub.cfm?articleid=1030240.

Broughton, V. (2006) The Need for a Faceted Classification as the Basis of all Methods of Information Retrieval, *Aslib Proceedings: New Information Perspectives*, **58** (1), 49–72.

Chowdhury, G. G., Poulter, A. and McMenemy, D. (2006) Public Library 2.0: towards a new mission for public libraries as a network of community knowledge, *Online Information Review*, **30** (4), 454–60.

Clark, P. (n.d.) *Some Ongoing KBS/Ontology Projects and Groups*, www.cs.utexas.edu/users/mfkb/related.html.

Gilchrist, A. (2006) Structure and Function in Retrieval, *Journal of Documentation*, **62** (1), 21–9.

Haynes, D. (2004) *Metadata for Information Management and Retrieval*, Facet Publishing.

Kayo, D. (2005) Beyond Subject Headings: a structured information retrieval tool for interdisciplinary fields, *Library Resources and Technical Services*, **49** (4), 266–75.

Kent, R. E. (2003) The IFF Foundation for Ontological Knowledge Organization. In Williamson, N. and Beghtol, C. (eds), *Knowledge Organization and Classification in International Information Retrieval*, Haworth Information Press.

Kilner, K. (2004) The AustLit Gateway and Scholarly Bibliography: a specialist implementation of the FRBR, *Cataloguing and Classification Quarterly*, **39** (3/4), 87–102.

Lausen, H., Ding, Y., Stollberg, M., Fensel, D., Hernandez, R. L. and Han, S. K. (2005) Semantic Web Portals: state-of-the-art survey, *Journal of Knowledge Management*, **9** (5), 40–9.

Le Boeuf, P. (2004a) FRBR: hype or cure-all? Introduction, *Cataloguing and Classification Quarterly*, **39** (3/4), 1–13.

Le Boeuf, P. (2004b) Musical Works in the FRBR Model or 'Quasi la Stessa Cosa': variations on a theme by Umberto Eco, *Cataloguing and Classification Quarterly*, **39** (3/4), 103–24.

Le Boeuf, P. (ed.) (2005) *Functional Requirements for Bibliographic Records (FRBR): hype or cure-all?,* Haworth Press.

Mai, J.-E. (2003) The Future of General Classification. In Williamson, N. and Beghtol, C. (eds), *Knowledge Organization and Classification in International Information Retrieval*, Haworth Information Press.

Miller, D. and Le Boeuf, P. (2004) 'Such stuff as dreams are made on': how does FRBR fit performing arts? *Cataloguing and Classification Quarterly*, **39** (3/4).

Mitchell, A. E. and Surratt, B. E. (2005) *Cataloging and Organizing Digital Resources*, Facet Publishing.

Nicolas, Y. (2004) Folklore Requirements for Bibliographic Records: oral traditions and FRBR, *Cataloguing and Classification Quarterly*, **39** (3/4), 179–95.

OCLC (2006a) *Automatic Classification Research at OCLC*, www.oclc.org/research/projects/auto_class/default.htm.

OCLC (2006b) *Scorpion*, www.oclc.org/research/software/scorpion/default.htm.

OCLC (2006c) *Terminology Services*, www.oclc.org/research/projects/termservices/default.htm.

Prokopiadou, G., Papatheodorou, P. and Moschopoulos, D. (2004) Integrating Knowledge Management Tools for Government Information, *Government Information Quarterly*, **21** (2), 170–98.

Reynolds, D., Shabajee, P. and Cayzer, S. (2004) *Semantic Information Portals*, www2004.org/proceedings/docs/2p290.pdf.

Shankaranarayanan, G. and Even, A. (2006) The Metadata Enigma, *Communications of the ACM*, **49** (2), 88–95.

Steffen, S. and Maedche, A. (2001) Knowledge Portals Ontologies at Work, *AI Magazine*, **22** (2), 63–75.

Stillone, P. (2004) The Future of Cataloguing, *Ariadne*, www.ariadne.ac.uk/issue40/cilip-cig-rpt/.

Sure, Y. and Studer, R. (2005) Semantic Web Technologies for Digital Libraries, *Library Management*, **26** (4/5), 190–5.

Tillett, B. (2005) *FRBR and Cataloguing Rules: impact on IFLA's statement of principles and AACR/RDA*, www.oclc.org/research/events/frbr-workshop/program.htm.

Vizine-Goetz, D. (2004) Terminology Services: making knowledge organization schemes more accessible to people and computers, *OCLC Newsletter*, www.oclc.org/news/publications/newsletters/oclc/2004/266/downloads/research.pdf.

Vizine-Goetz, D., Hickey, C., Houghton, A. and Thompson, R. (2004) Vocabulary Mapping for Terminology Services, *Journal of Digital Information*, **4** (4), http://jodi.ecs.soton.ac.uk/articles/v04/i04/vizine-goetz/ .

Zhang, J. and Jastram, I. (2006) A Study of the Metadata Creation Behavior of Different User Groups on the Internet, *Information Processing and Management*, **42** (4), 1099–122.

# Index

subject gateways 2, 111
  *see also* Intute: arts & humanities; Intute:
    health & life sciences; Intute: social
    sciences
subject heading 18
subject heading lists 13, 18, 19, 34,
    111–29, 171
  and thesauri: differences 112–13
  definition 112
  limitations for indexing internet
    resources 135–6
  use in organization of internet
    resources 122
subject indexing 4, 112
  post-coordinate 112
  pre-coordinate 112

taxonomy 4, 24, 173–4
TEI 1151
term similarities 20
Text Encoding Initiative *see* TEI
thesaurus 4, 18, 19, 112, 113, 116–22, 171
  alphabetical display121
  definition 116–17
  relationships 118–20
    associative relationship 118, 120
    equivalence relationship 118–9
    hierarchical relationship 118, 119–20
  terms, display 121–2
  use in organization of internet resources
    122

UDC 71, 77, 99–103
  auxiliary tables 100
  building numbers 102–3
  common auxiliaries 100
  features 99
  main classes 100
  special signs 101–102
UF
  in thesaurus 115, 119
UKMARC 54, 60
UNESCO thesaurus 122
Unified Medical Language System
    (UMLS) 175
uniform resource identifier *see* URI
uniform resource locator *see* URL

uniform resource name *see* URN
UNIMARC 47, 49, 60–3
  field types 62–6
  history 66
  record 53
Universal Decimal Classification *see* UDC
URI 4, 26, 136, 201–2, 203
  vs. URL and URN 201–2
.URIrefs 203, 204
URL 2, 60, 202
URN 202
used for *see* UF
user-driven classification 220–1
USMARC 54, 60

Virtua 214
Vivisimo 2, 23
vocabulary control tools 4, 18, 23, 111,
    128
  definition 111–12

web 17, 18
  directory 23, 25
  information organization 22
  information resources: characteristics
    131–3
  search tools 4
  user-driven classification 220–1
WebDewey 96–8
  features 96
WebOnto 178
Web Ontology Language *see* OWL
WordNet 24, 175

XHTML 159
XML 26, 136, 161–5, 201
  characteristics 163–4
  vs. XML 162–3
XML documents 164–5
XML schema 4, 166–7

Yahoo! 2
*Yellow Pages* 3, 5

UNIVERSITY OF WALES NEWPORT LIBRARY AND INFORMATION SERVICES CAERLEON